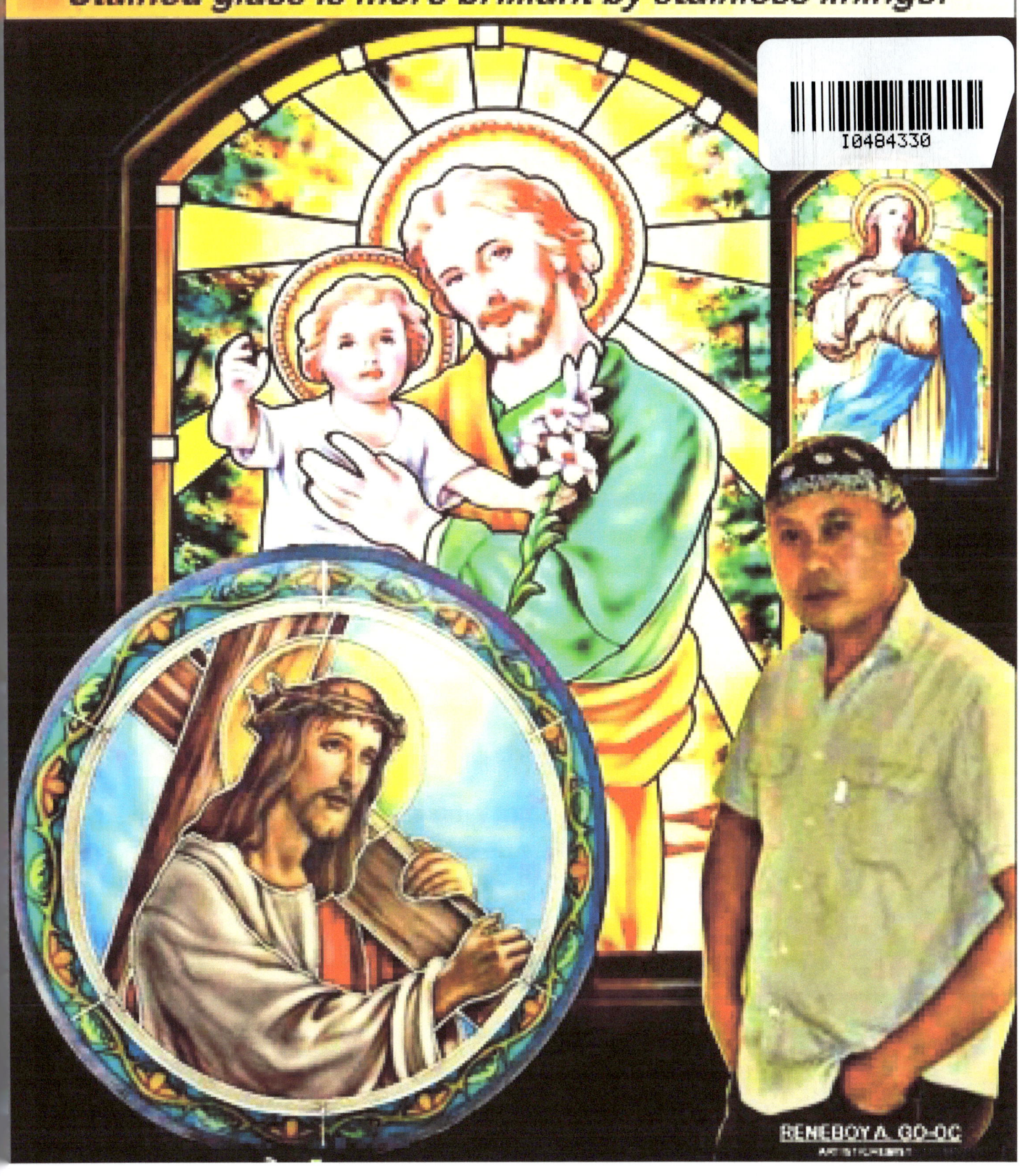

REGO STAINED GLASS

Branch 1; # 554 Liparo Street, Bagong Barrio, Caloocan City   Branch 2; #56 Rizal Street, Manaoag, Pangasinan

Cell # 0939 363 9682   0918 733 8385

Stained glass is more brilliant by stainless linings!

I0484330

BENEBOY A. GO-OC
ARTIST/CHEMIST

REGO ARTWORKS
BY
RENE BOY A. GO-OC, ARTIST

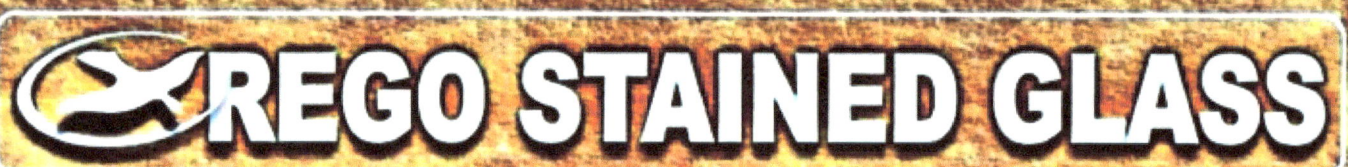

REGO STAINED GLASS

Main; Leparo Street, Bagong Barrio, Caloocan City   Branch; #56 Rizal Street, Manaoag, Pangasnan

0939 363 9682

Stained glass is more brilliant by stainless linings!

REGO STAINED GLASS now discover the best and guaranteed stained glass over produced in this generation. All colors never fades because it was heated in oven to capture long lasting color harmony and a glass with durability than ever because it is made of fiber glass.

We use stainless lining to indicate uniqueness of design and stronger than led. We offer unique special stained glass that are made of led and glass to our budget oriented clients. We can also offer a minimum price of a back to back panel laminated finish with fiber glass. Its low cost features also be protected with durability. Either of these packages, We binds guarantee to answer your satisfaction.

Published by Tatay Jobo Elizes.
Printed in USA under the following ISBN Codes:
ISBN-13: 978 - 1503170612   ISBN-10: 1503170616

Publisher: **Tatay Jobo Elizes** was born in Manila, Philippines, in 1934, retiree, now based in NY, busy self-publishing and involved in piglets dispersal programs.

Acknowledgement & Dedication: Gratitude and acknowledgment belongs to those who support my hobby publishing books and charities.

I heartily dedicate this book to my wife, **Cora**, my children, **Tetchie, Chevy & Abeth, and Marie & Bimbo,** my grandchildren, **Karines & Aung, Noelle, Chad, Marjo, Jeb, Marvin & Marty,** great-grandsons **Jason Win** and **Carson,** my siblings **Susan, Hilda, Bobby, Bey & Manny** and to all my **extended relatives and to all Filipinos.**

Publisher's List at last page - Contact job_elizes@yahoo.com, tatay@usa.com
My websites: http://tinyurl.com/mj76ccq + + + www.jobelizes.com
"Buy A Book or Gift Somebody - paperback or kindle edition online"

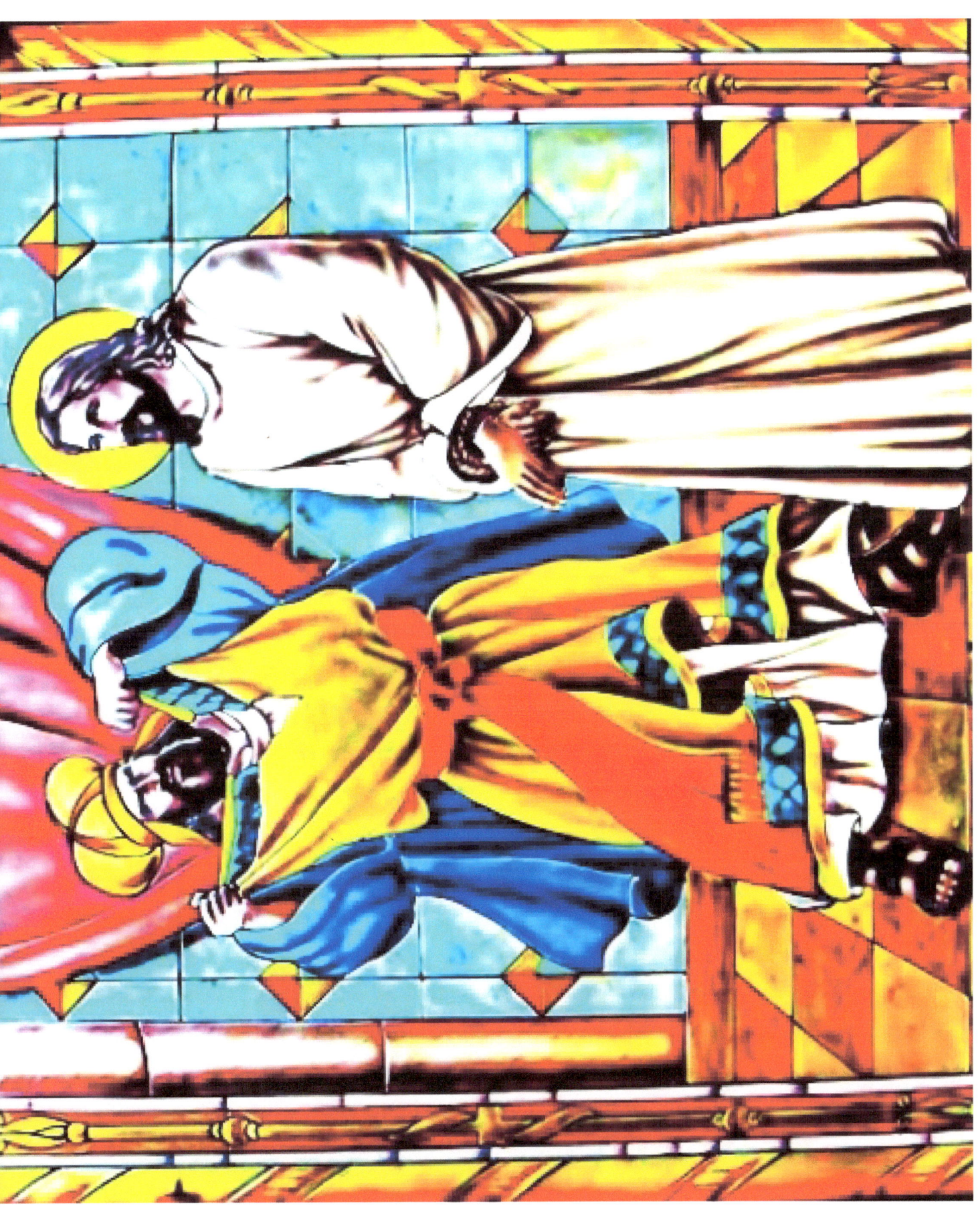

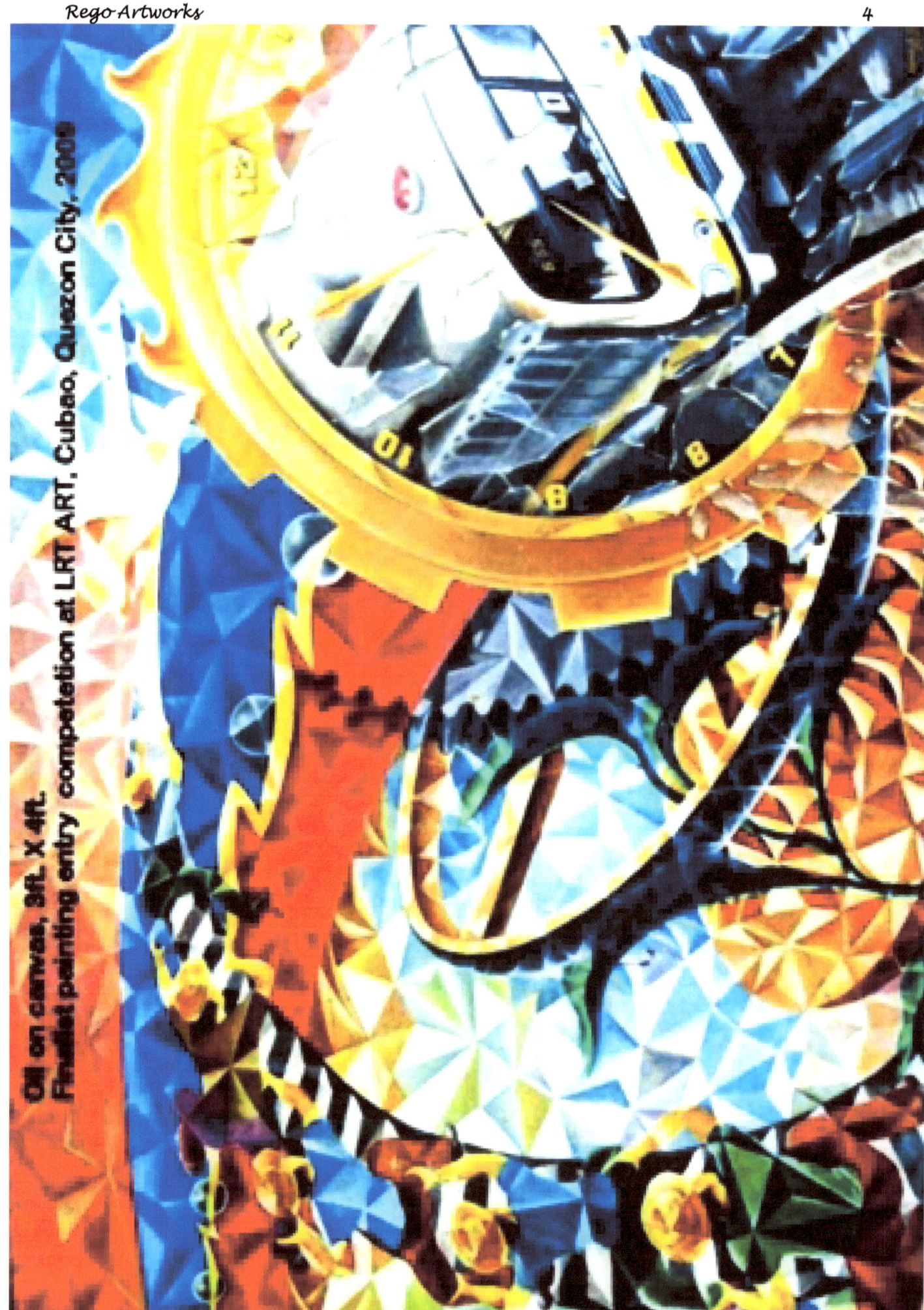

Oil on canvas, 3ft. X 4ft.
Finalist painting entry competetion at LRT ART, Cubao, Quezon City, 2009

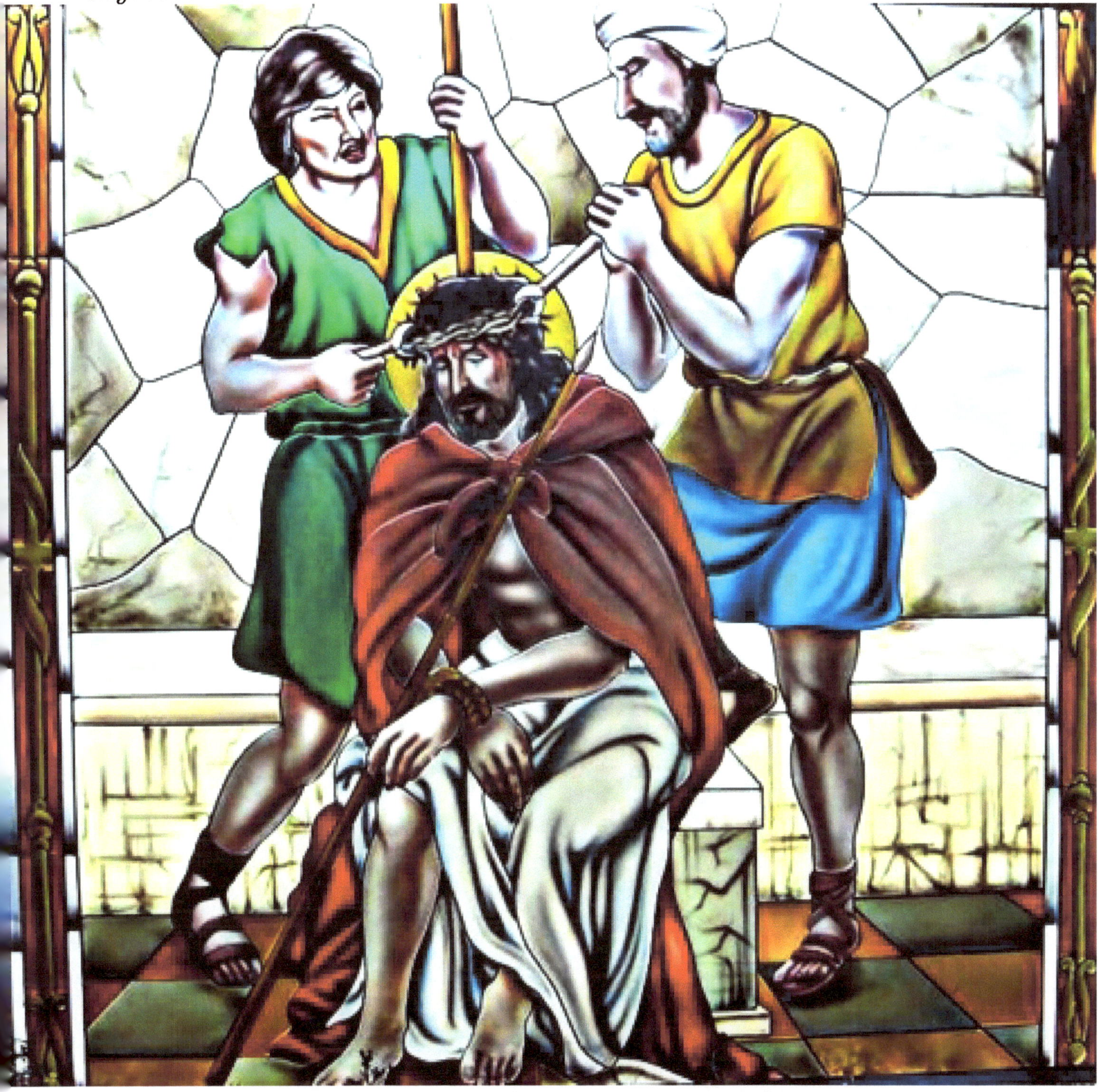

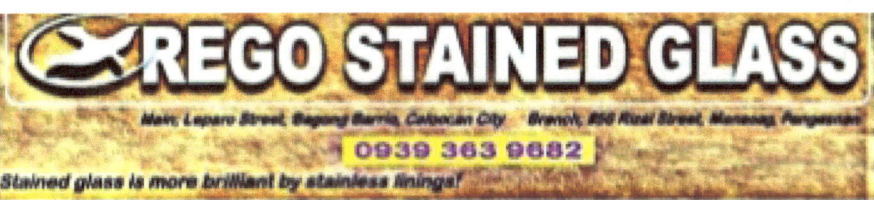

REGO STAINED GLASS

Main: Leparo Street, Bagong Barrio, Caloocan City · Branch: 826 Rizal Street, Manaoag, Pangasinan

0939 363 9882

Stained glass is more brilliant by stainless linings!

REGO STAINED GLASS now discover the best and guaranteed stained glass over produced in this generation. All colors never fades because it was heated in oven to capture long lasting color harmony and a glass with durability than ever because it is made of fiber glass.

We use stainless lining to indicate uniqueness of design and stronger than led. We offer unique special stained glass that are made of led and glass to our budget oriented clients. We can also offer a minimum price of a back to back panel laminated finish with fiber glass. Its low cost features also be protected with durability. Either of these packages, We binds guarantee to answer your satisfaction.

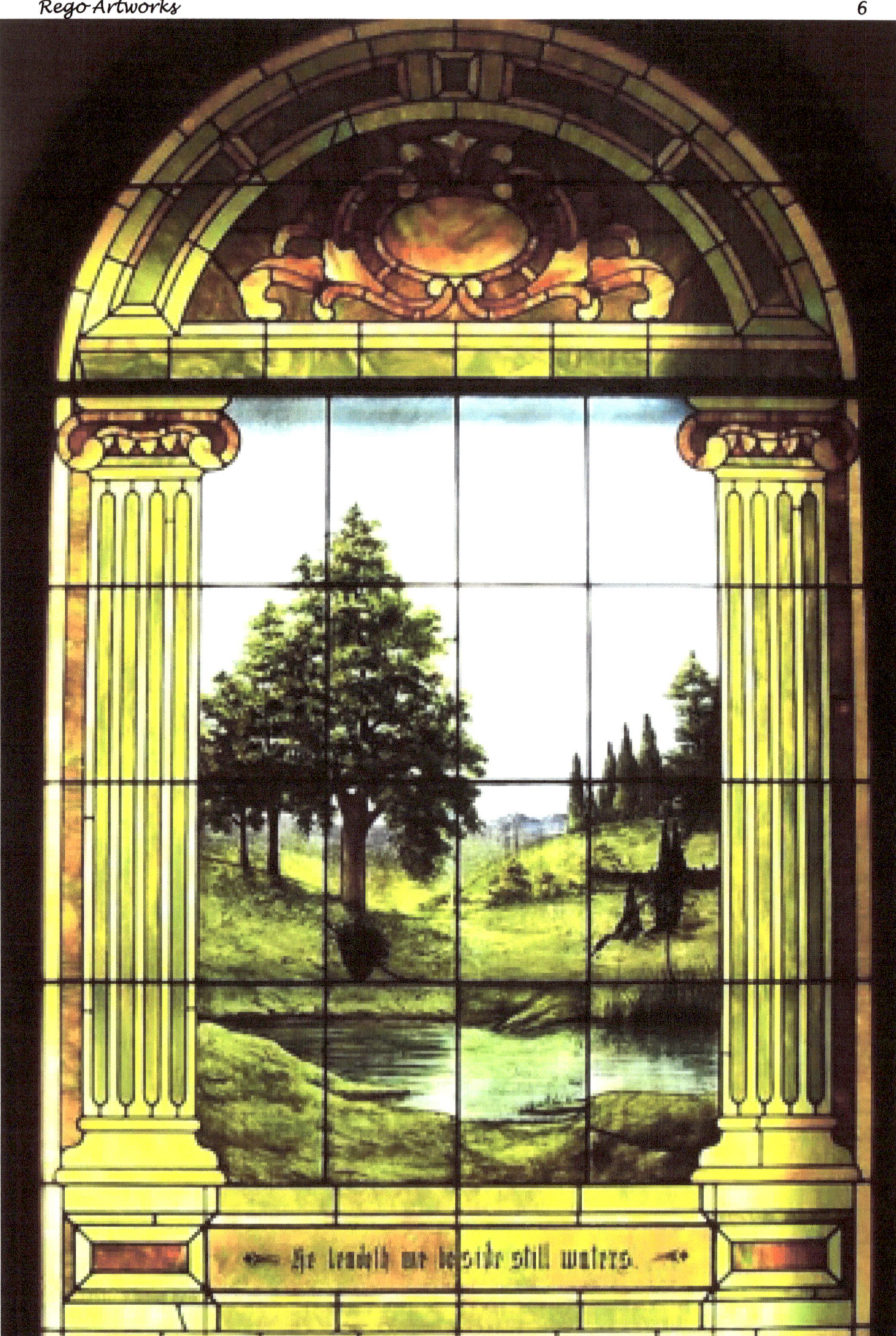

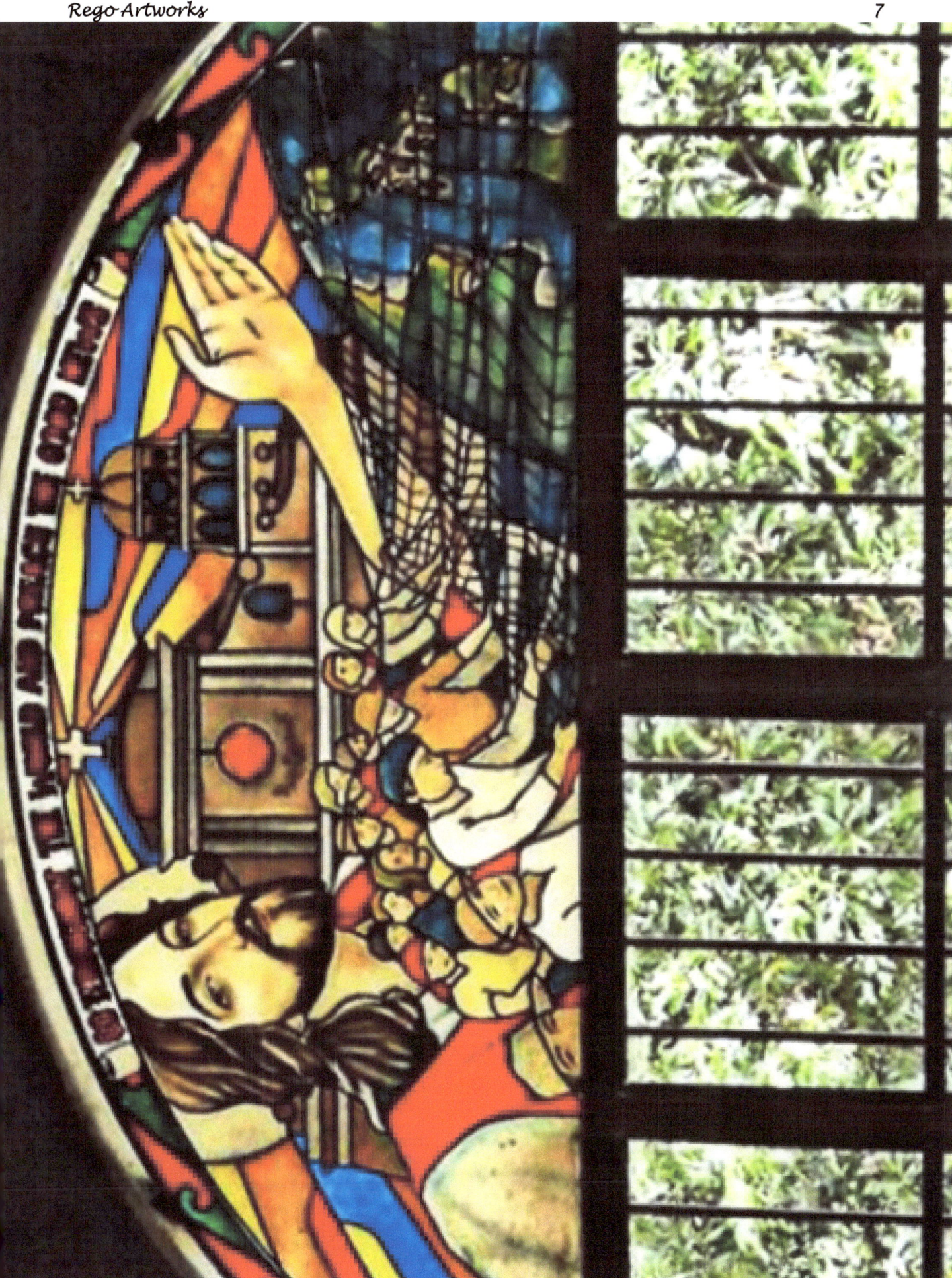

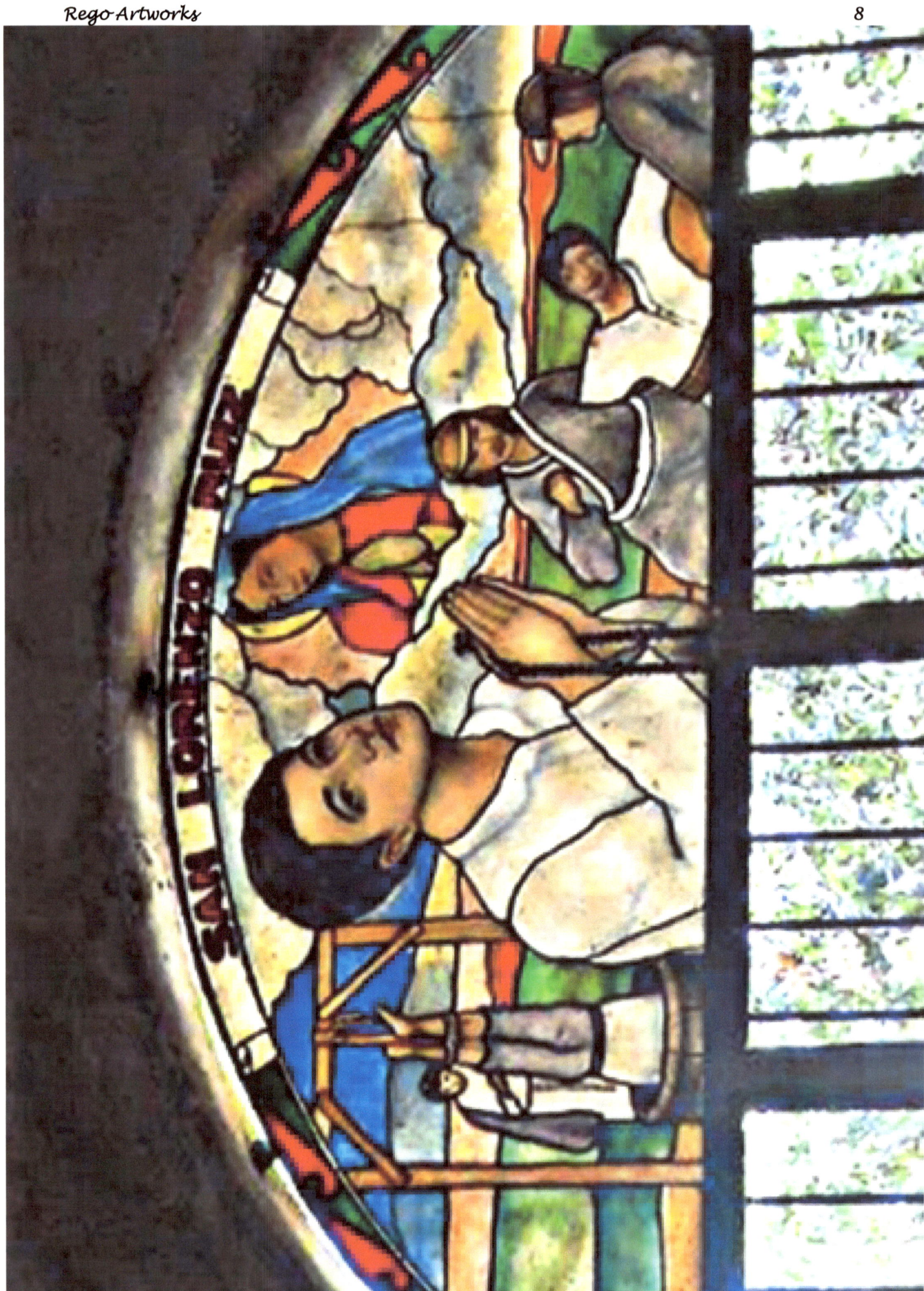

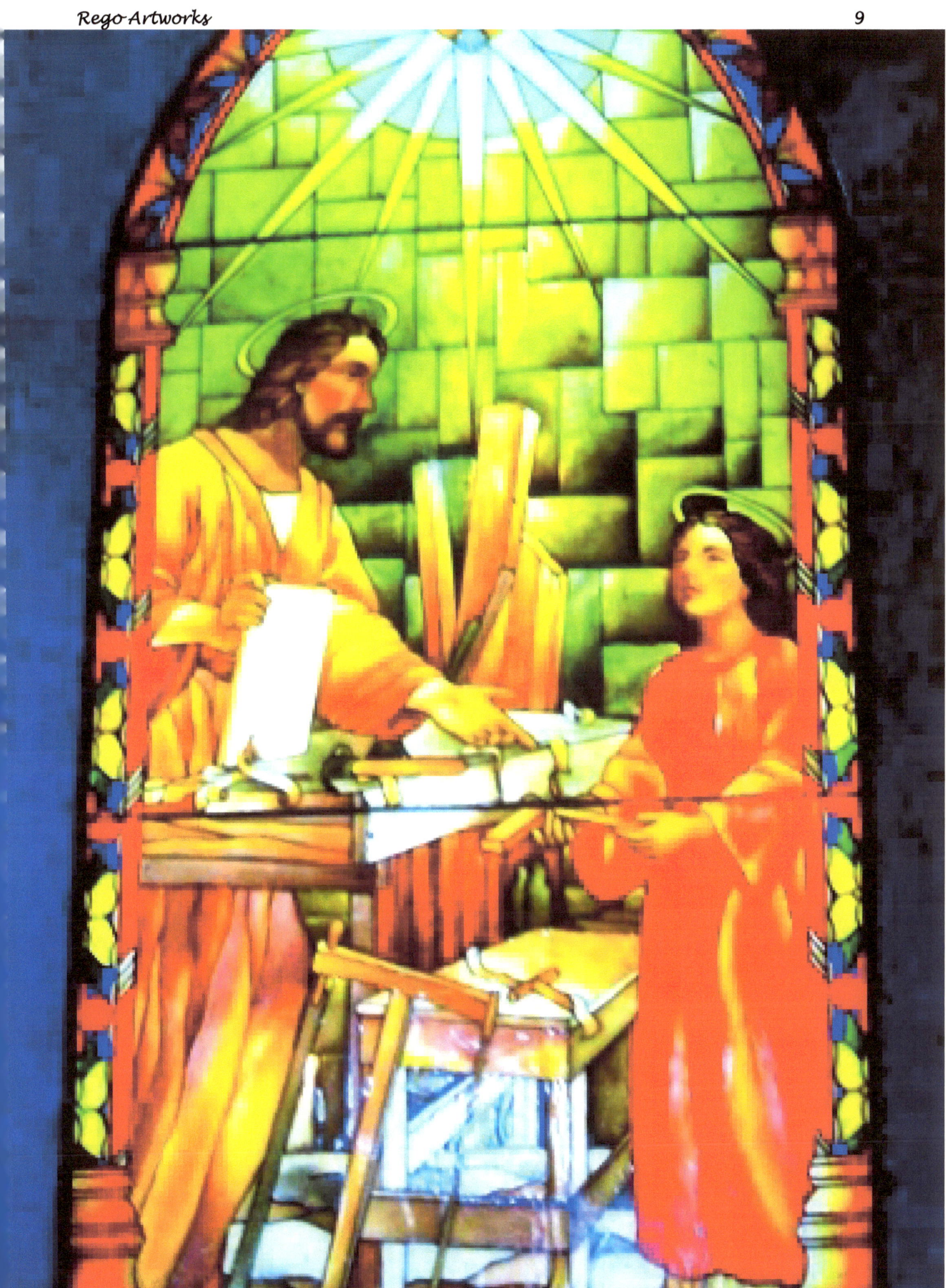

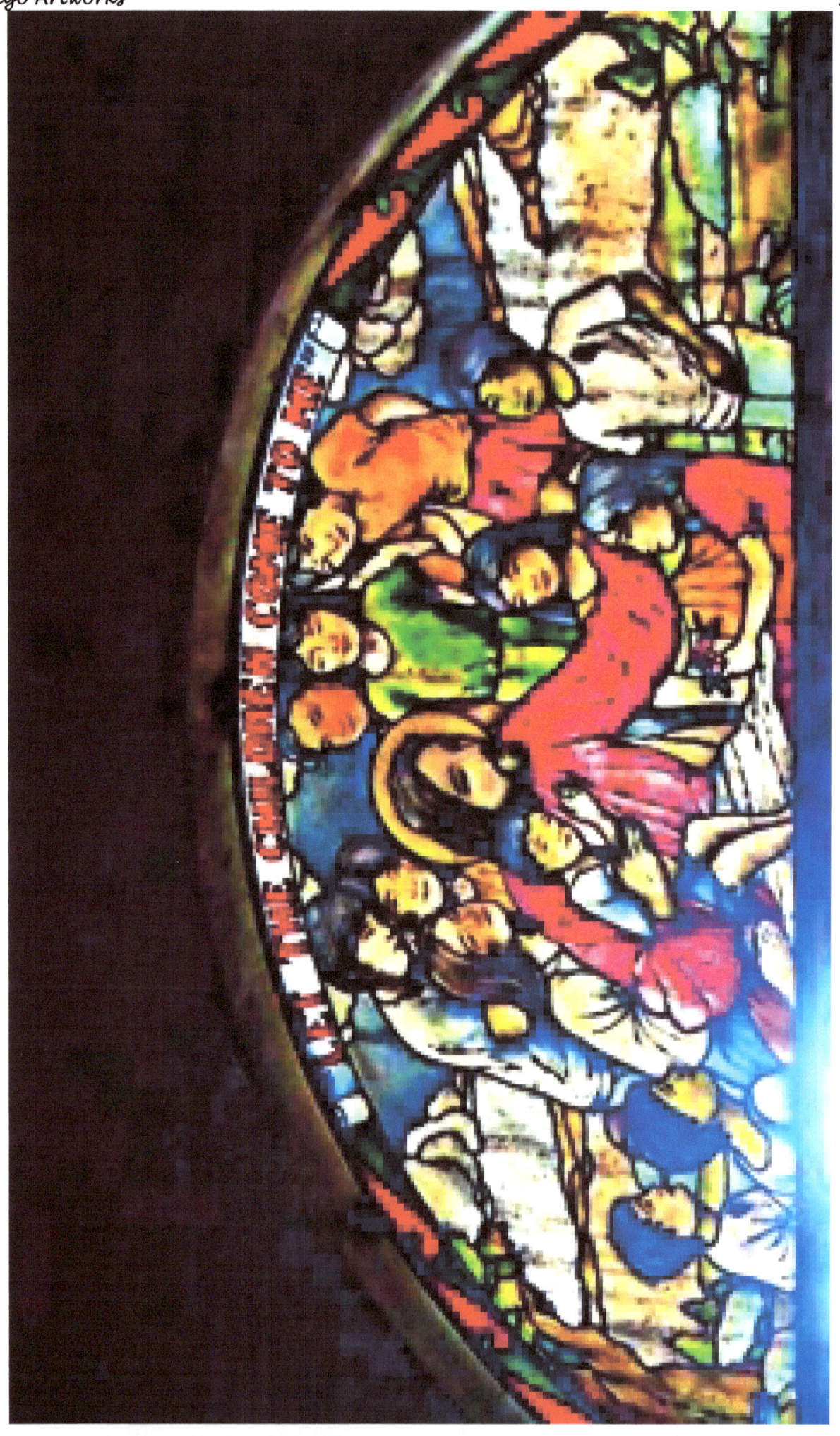

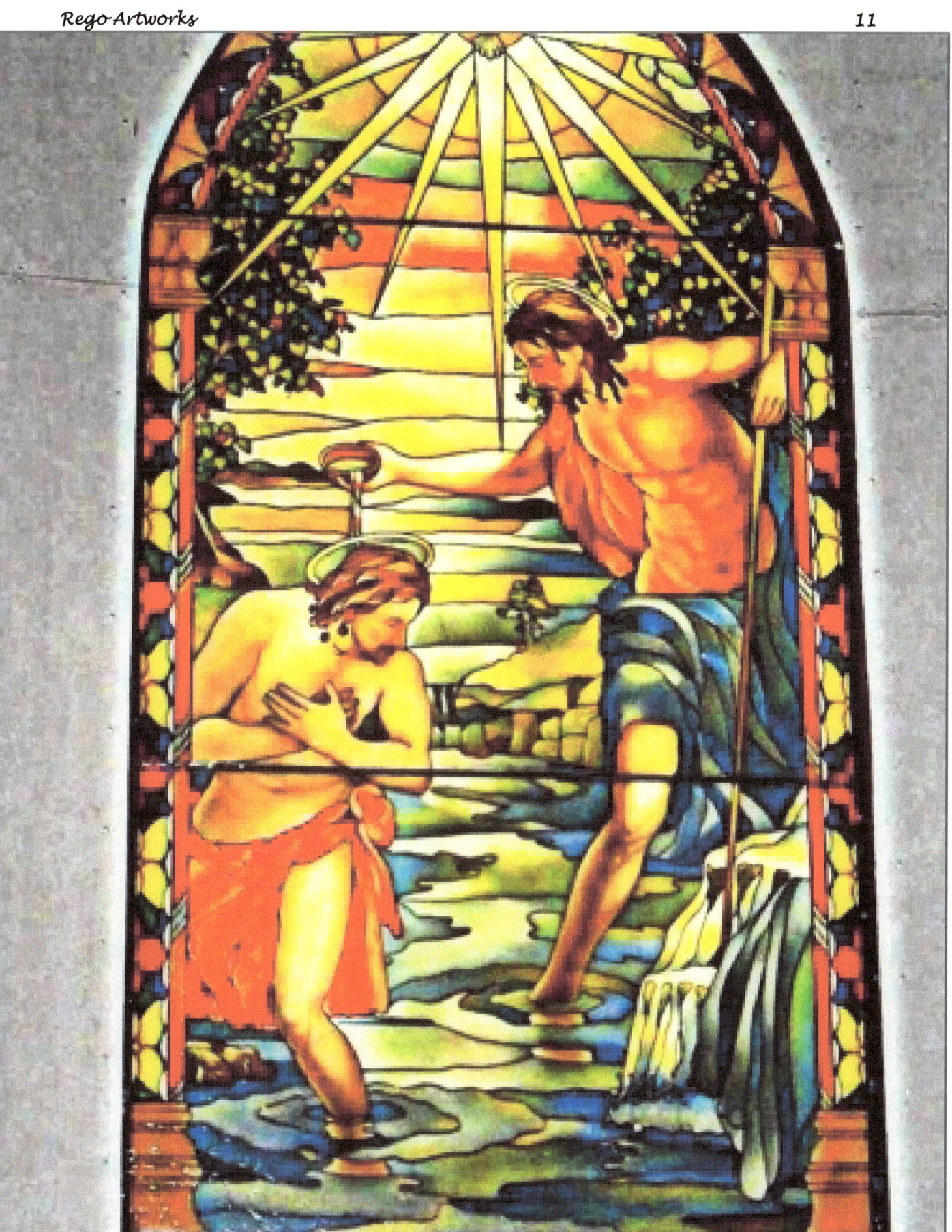

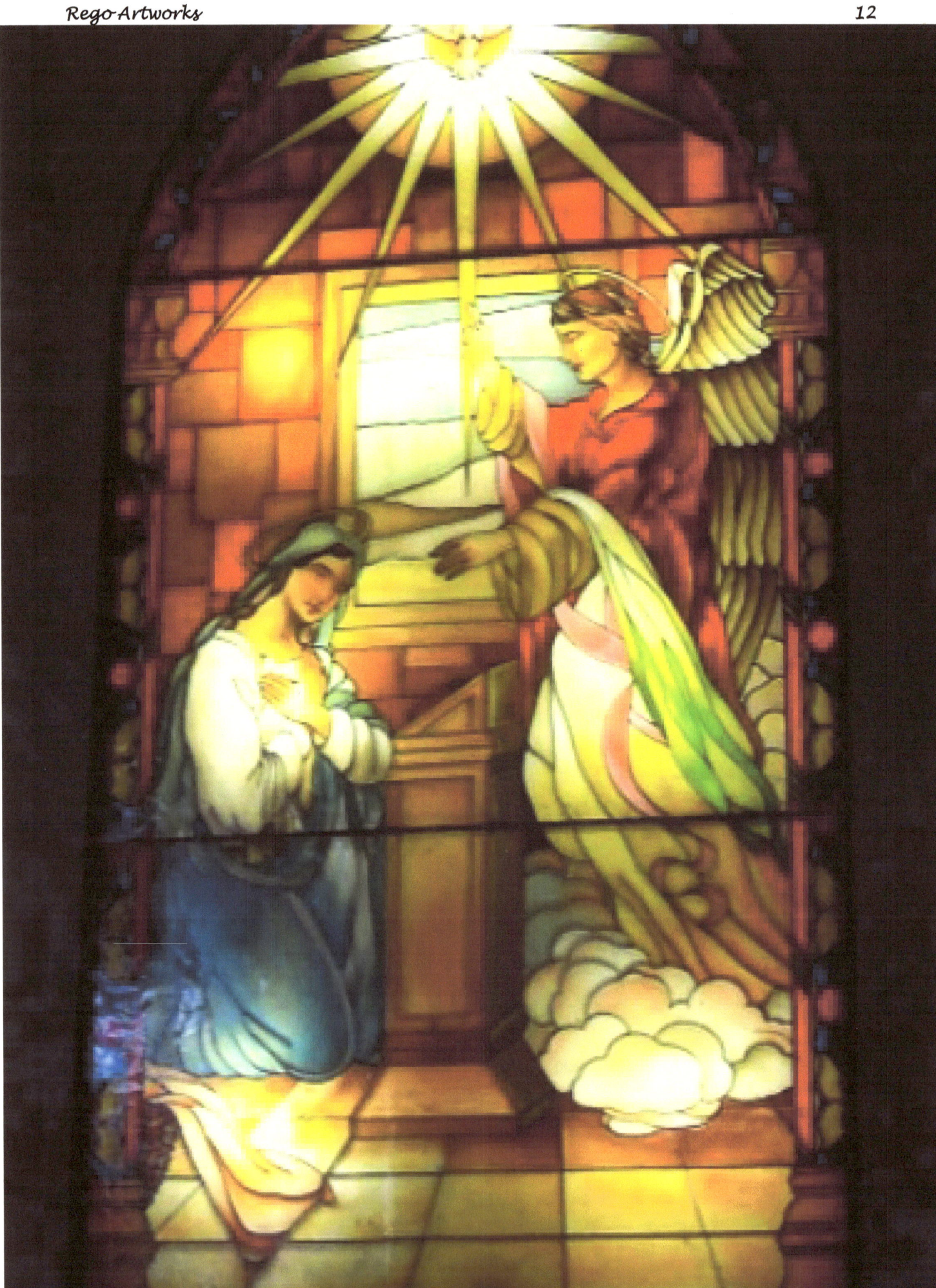

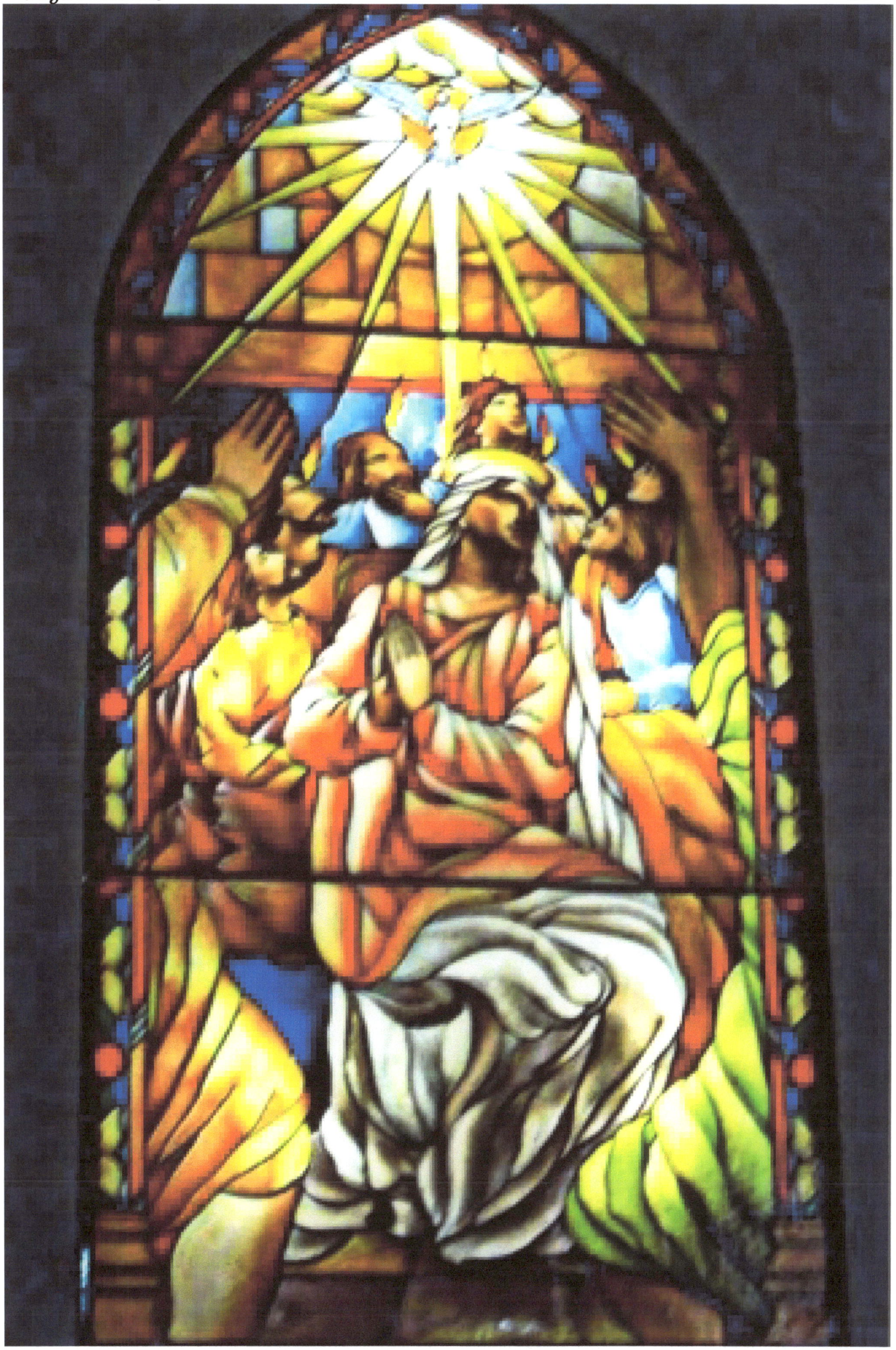

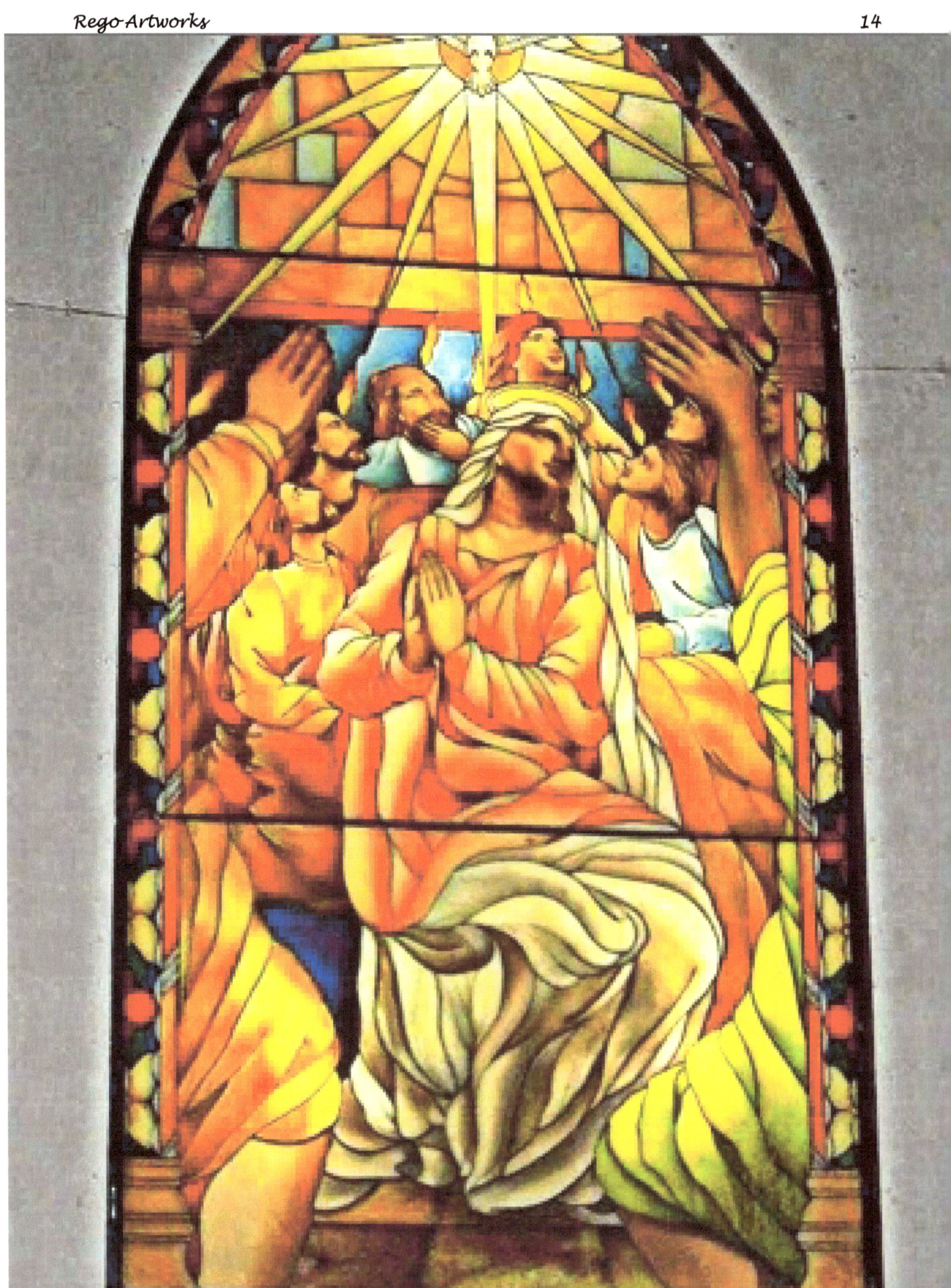

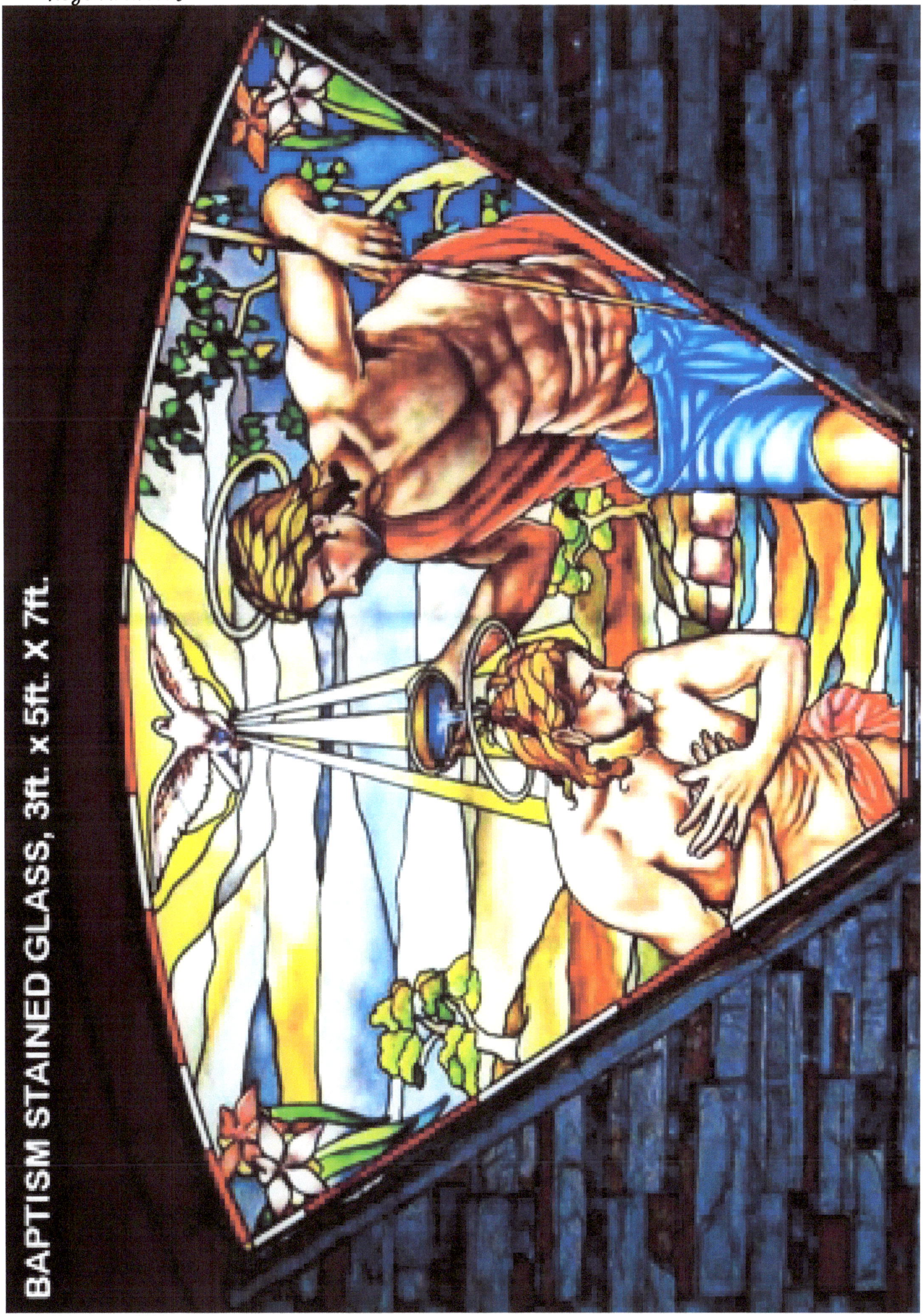

BAPTISM STAINED GLASS, 3ft. x 5ft. X 7ft.

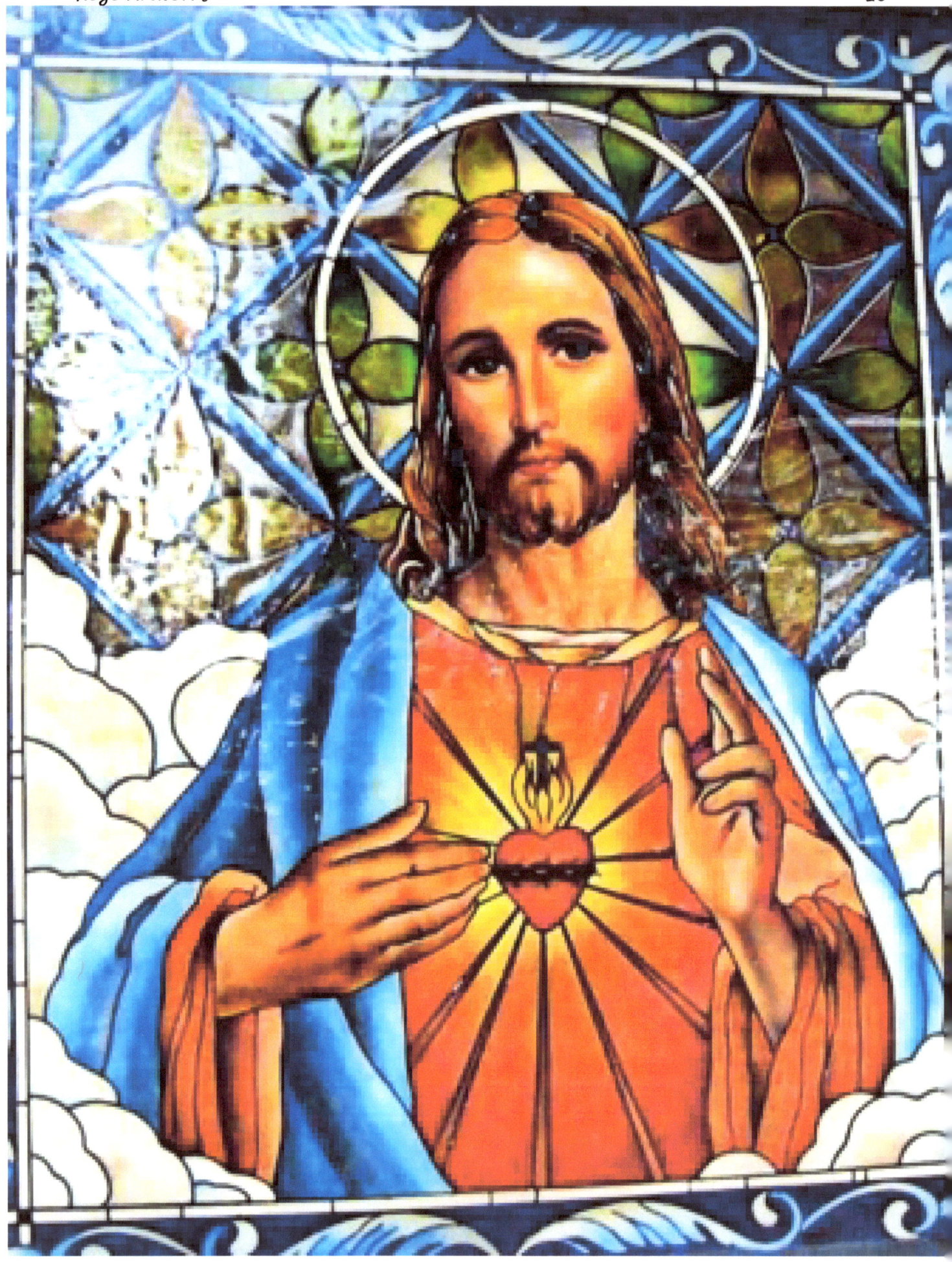

TWIN HEART STAINED GLASS, 4ft. X 5ft.

Bonuan Buqueg, Dagupan City, Pangasinan

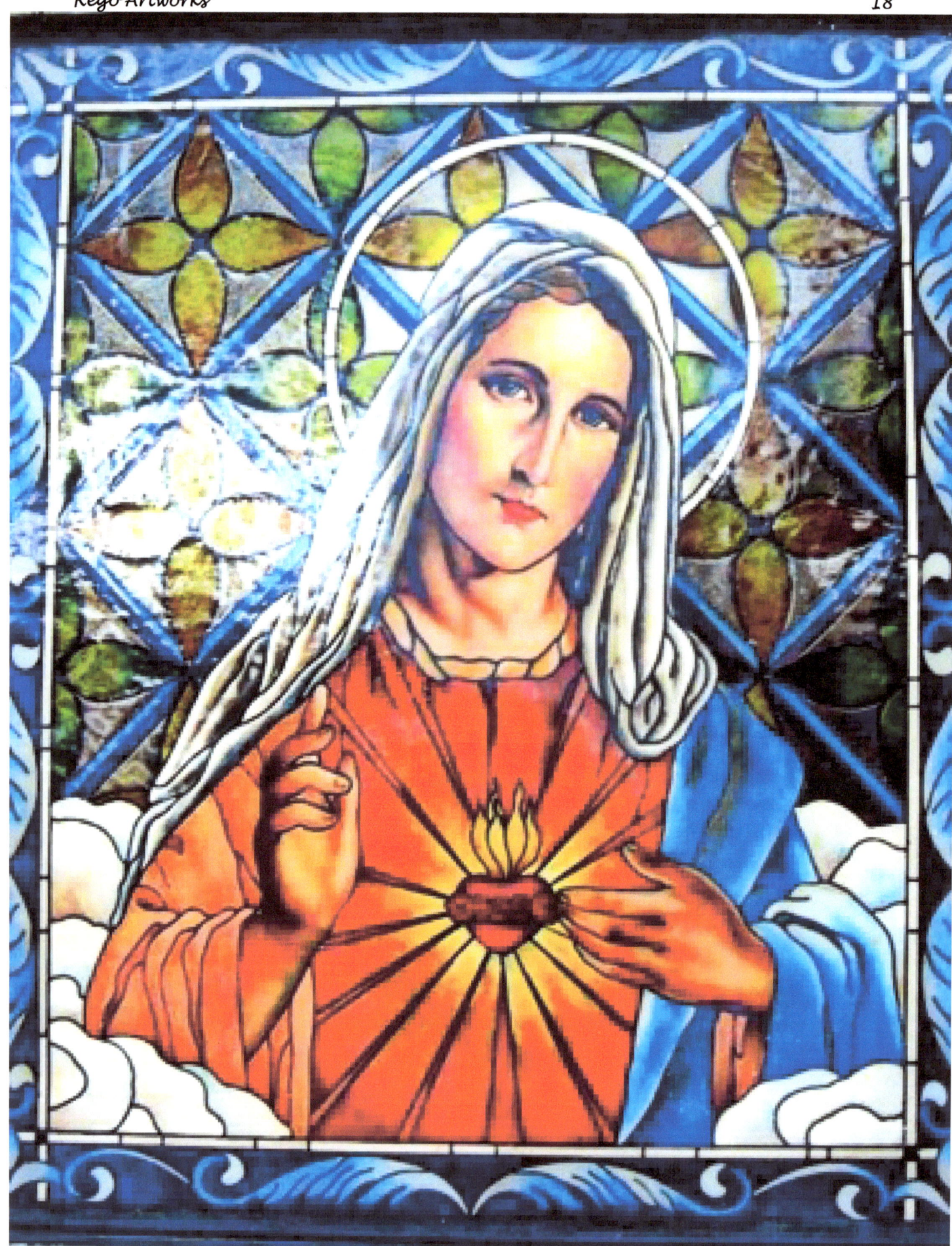

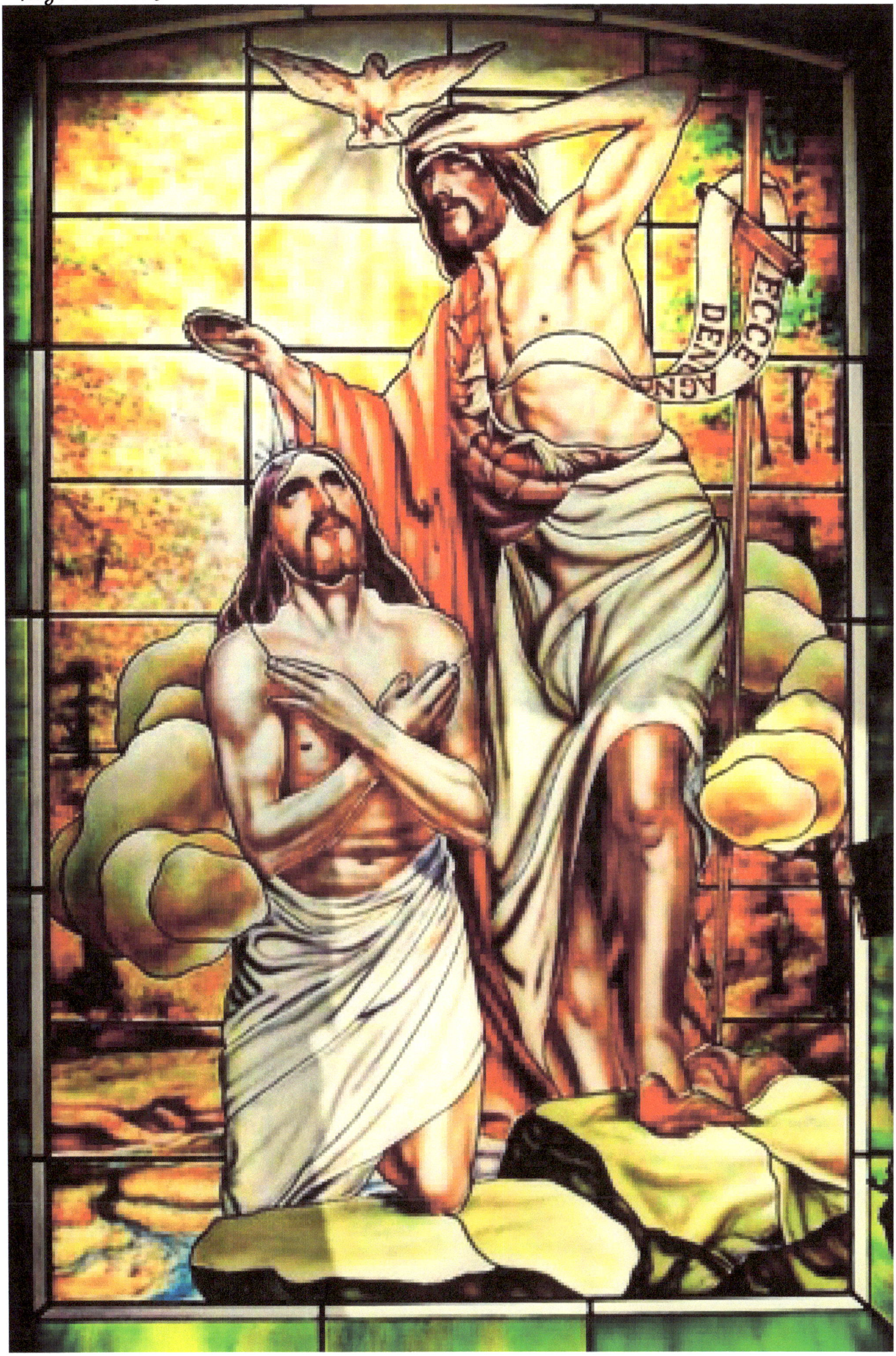
ECCE

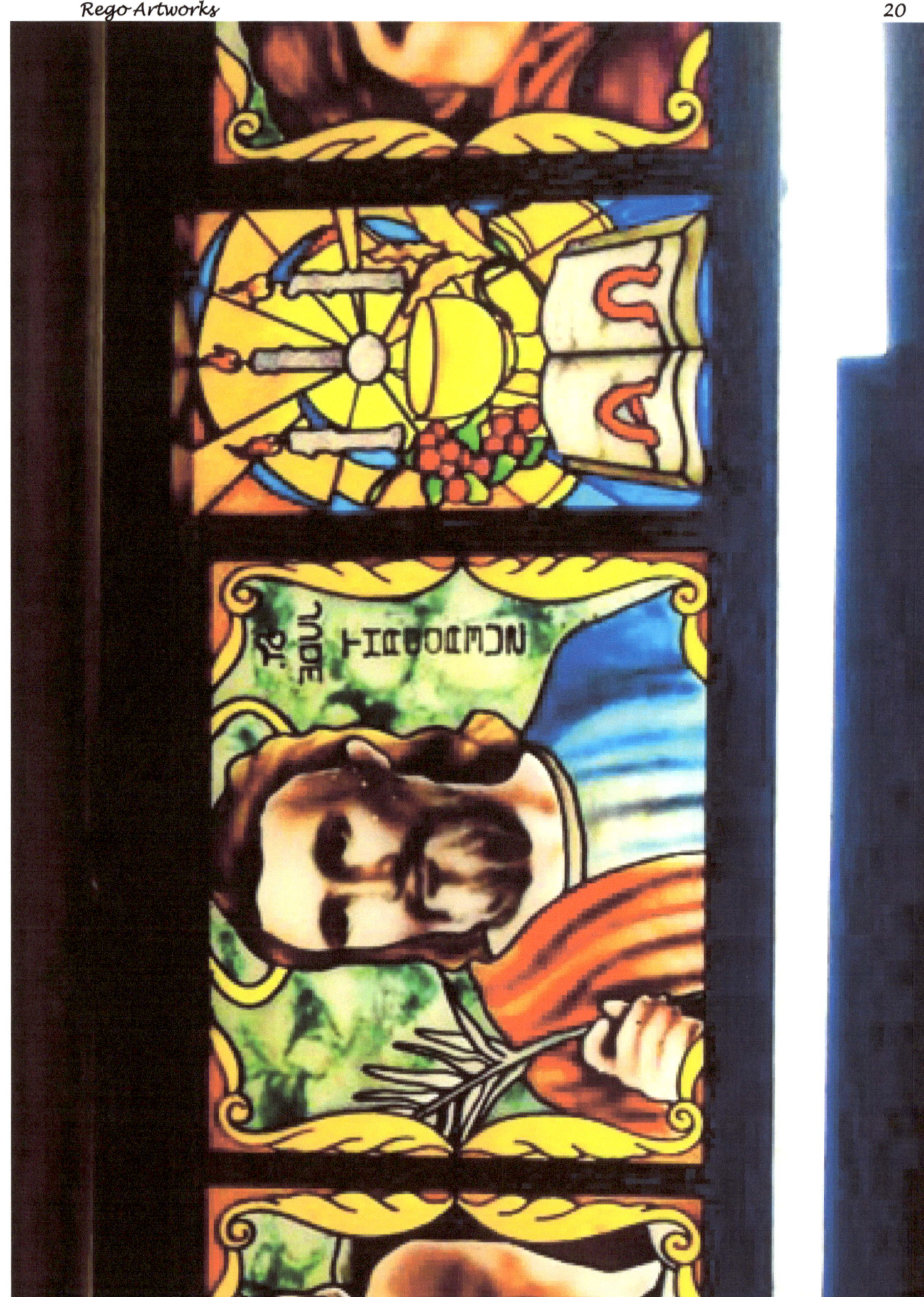

Oil on canvas, 2ft. x 6ft., FOUR GOSPEL

San Marcus

San Mateo

Holy Family Parish, Brgy., Tandoc, San Carlos City, Pangsinan

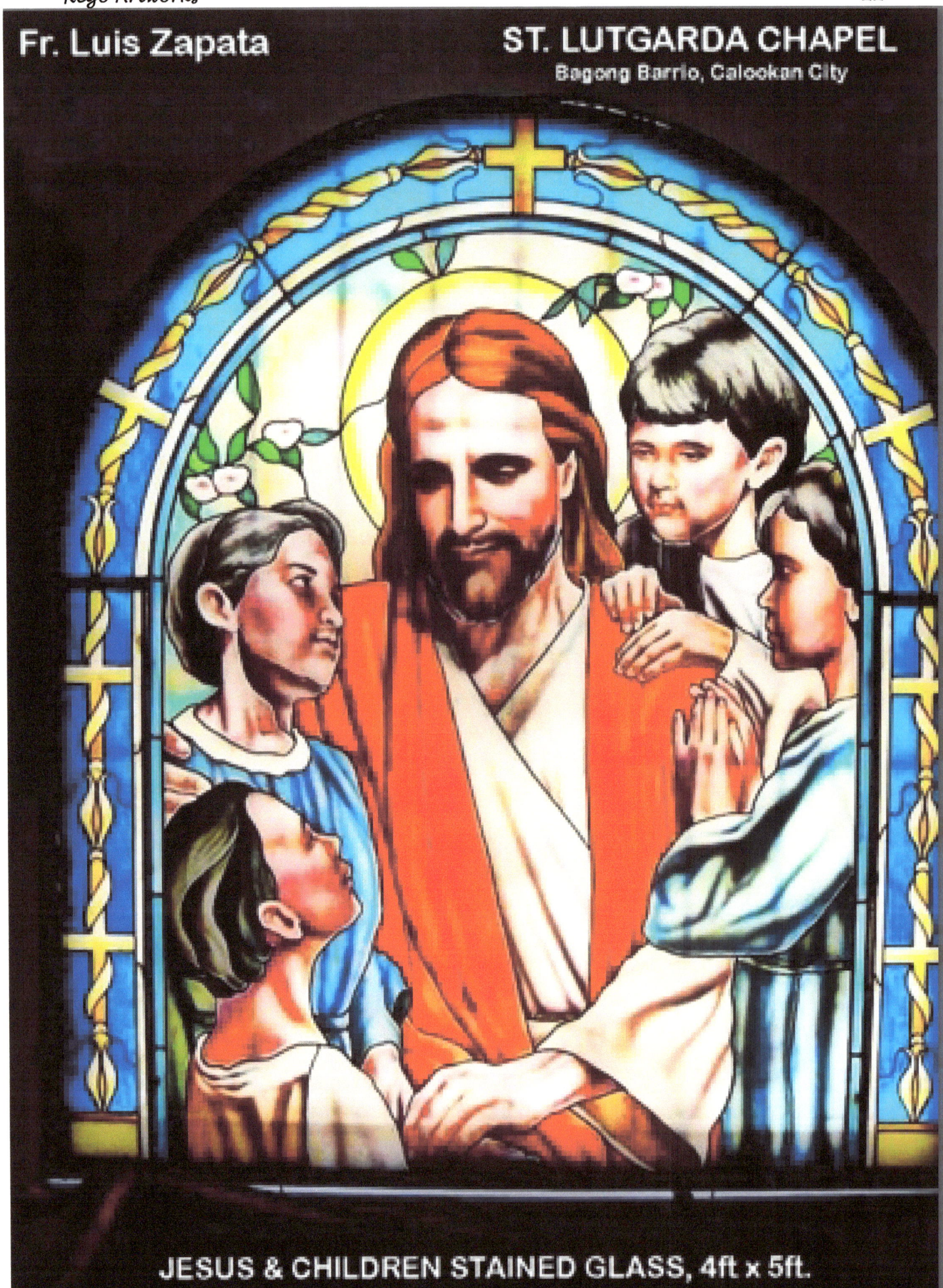

Fr. Luis Zapata

ST. LUTGARDA CHAPEL
Bagong Barrio, Caloocan City

JESUS & CHILDREN STAINED GLASS, 4ft x 5ft.

The Resurrection of Jesus Christ, stained glass-8ft. X 12ft.

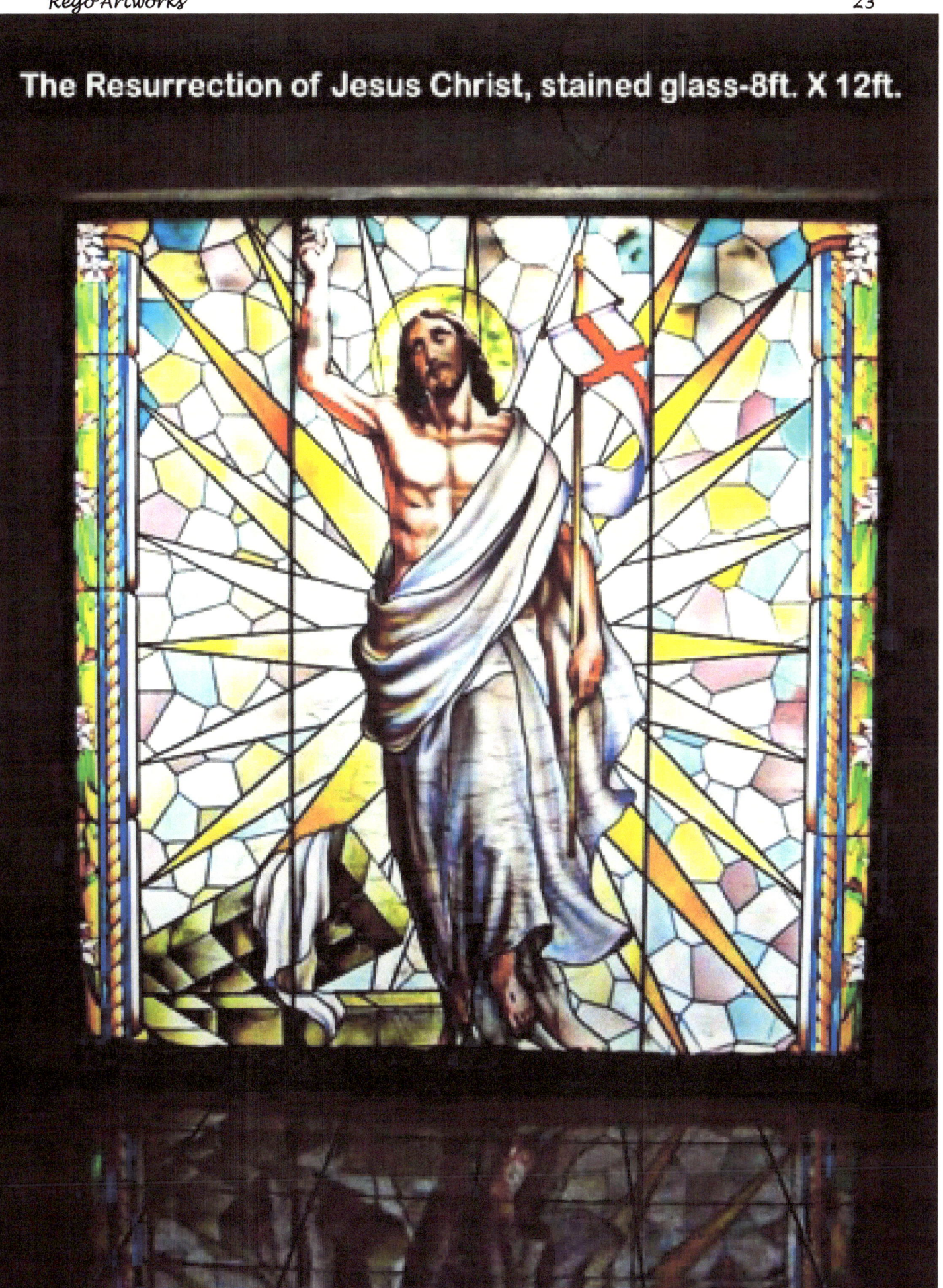

Oil on canvas, 2ft. *6ft., FOUR GOSPEL

San Juan

San Lucas

Holy Family Parish, Brgy., Tandoc, San Carlos City, Pangsinan

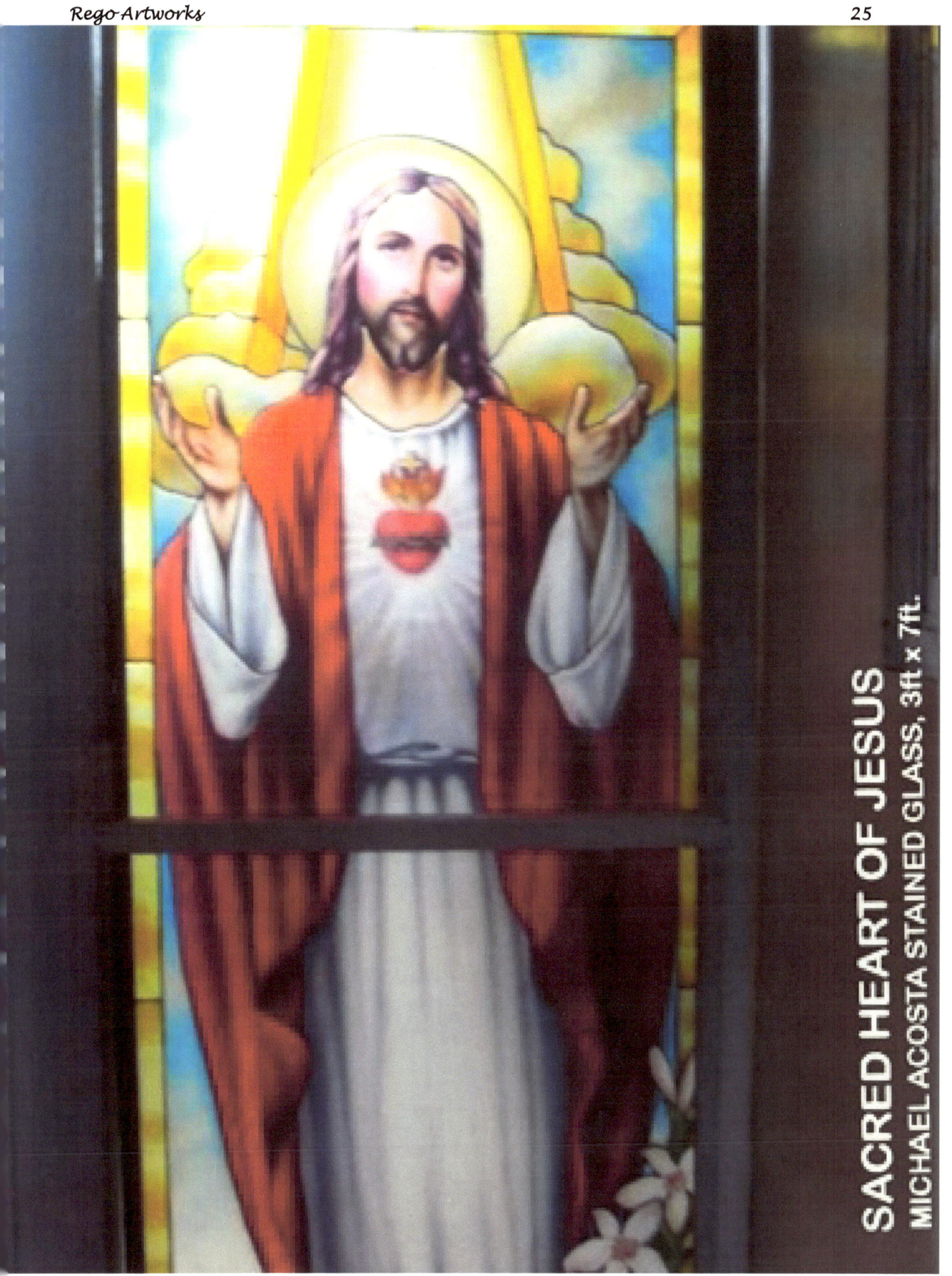

SACRED HEART OF JESUS
MICHAEL ACOSTA STAINED GLASS, 3ft x 7ft.

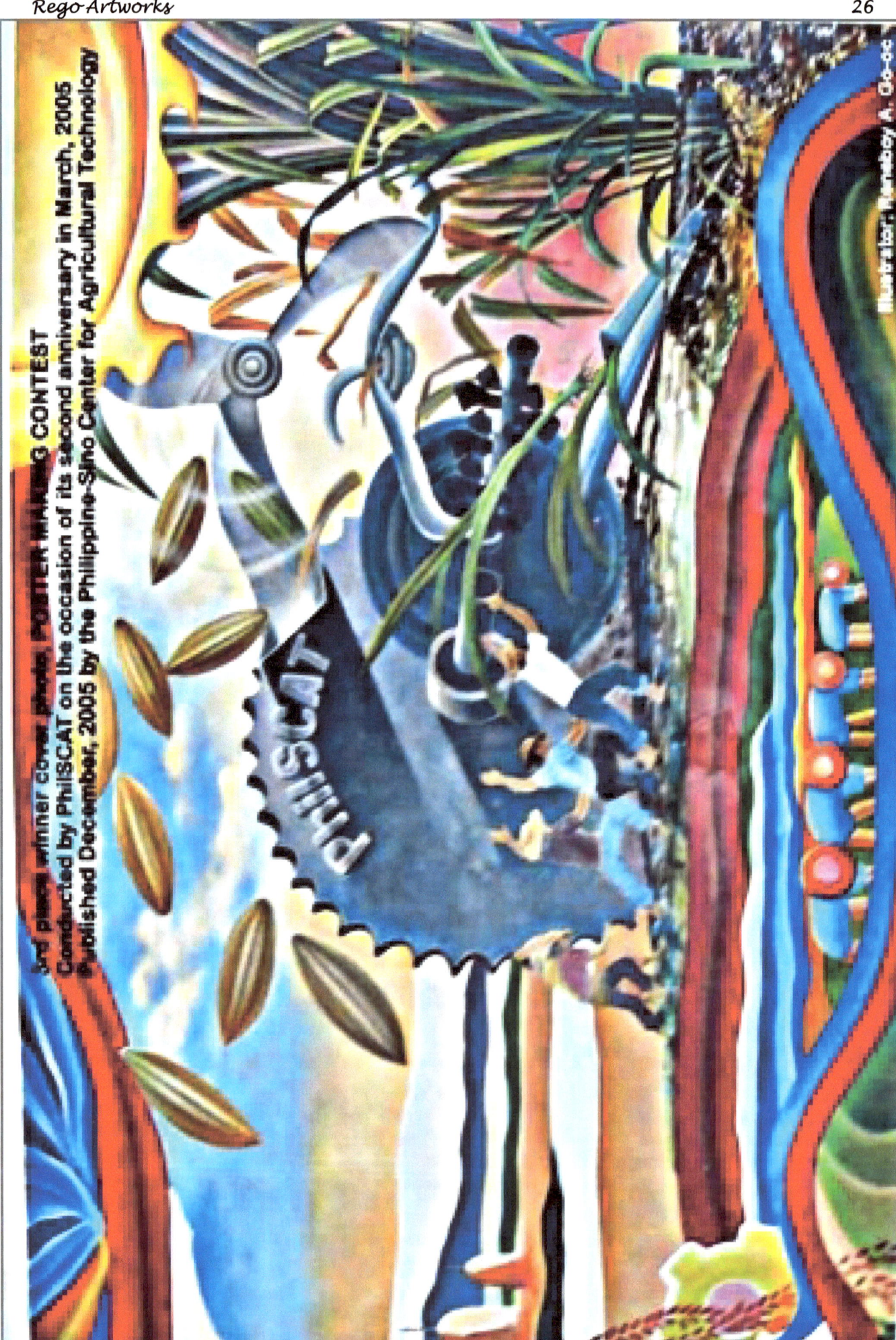

3rd place winner Cover photo, POSTER MAKING CONTEST
Conducted by PhilSCAT on the occasion of its second anniversary in March, 2005
Published December, 2005 by the Philippine-Sino Center for Agricultural Technology

Illustrator: Renzboy A. Go-oc

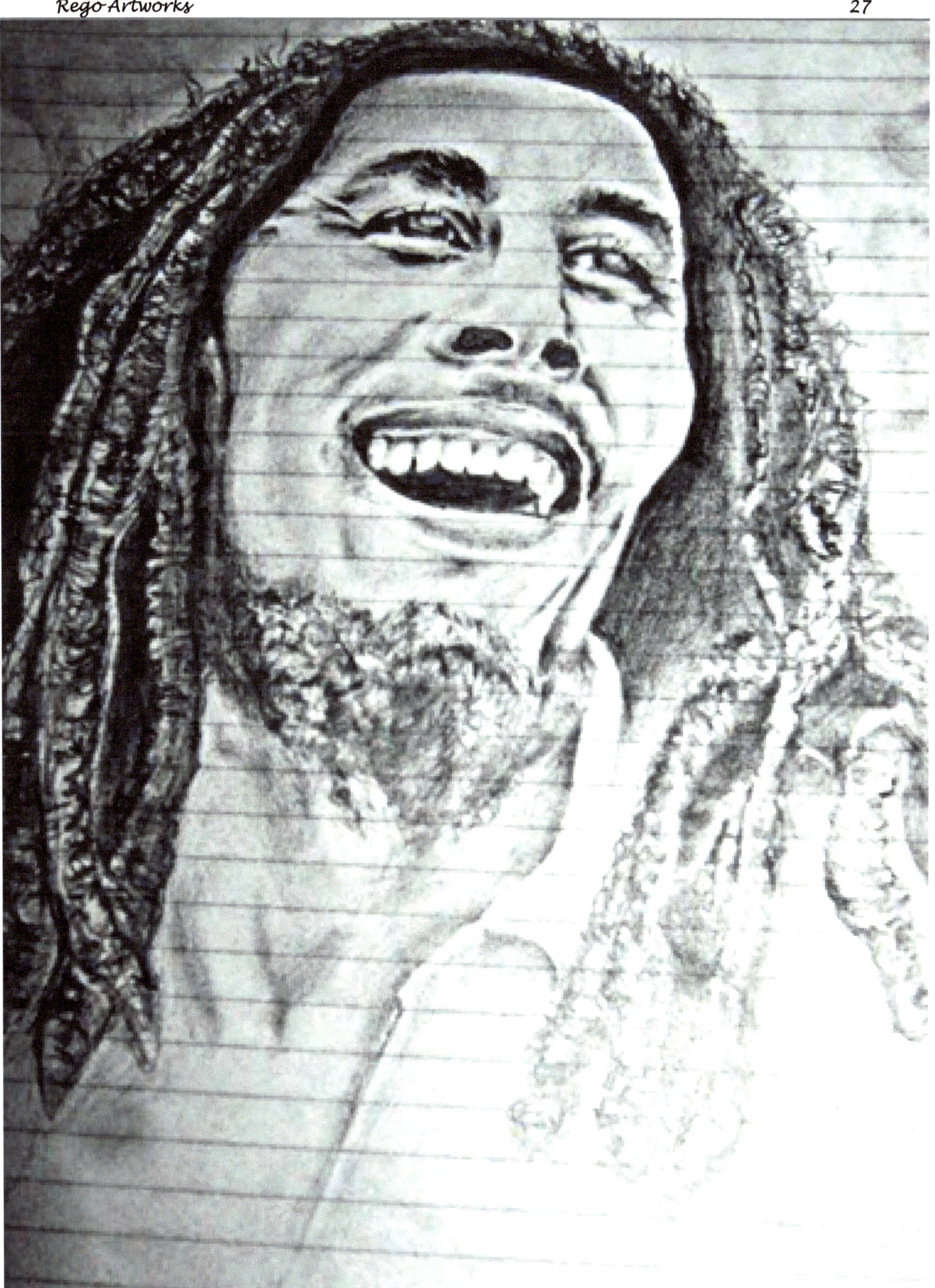

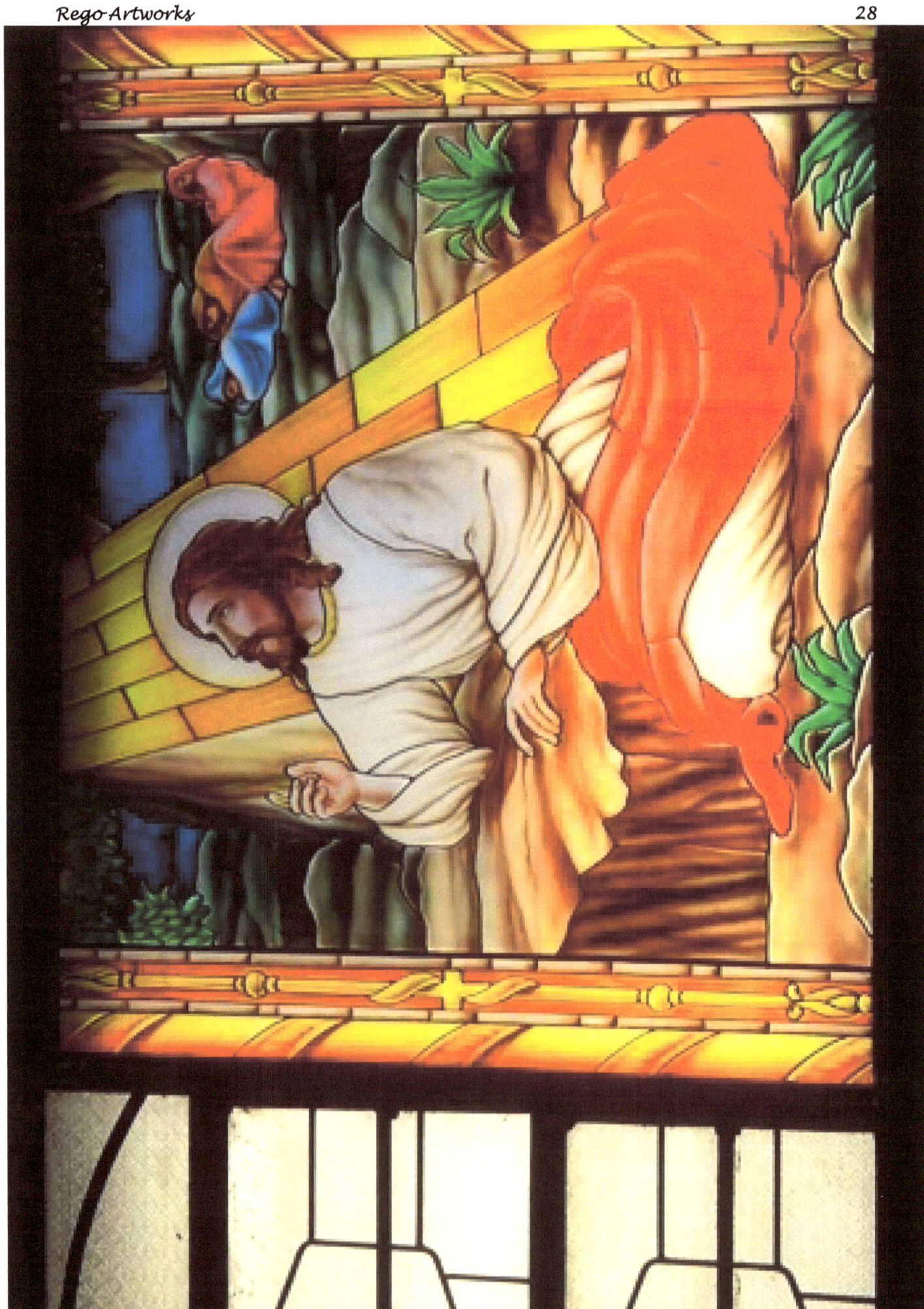

TWIN HEART STAINED GLASS, 6ft. X 11ft.

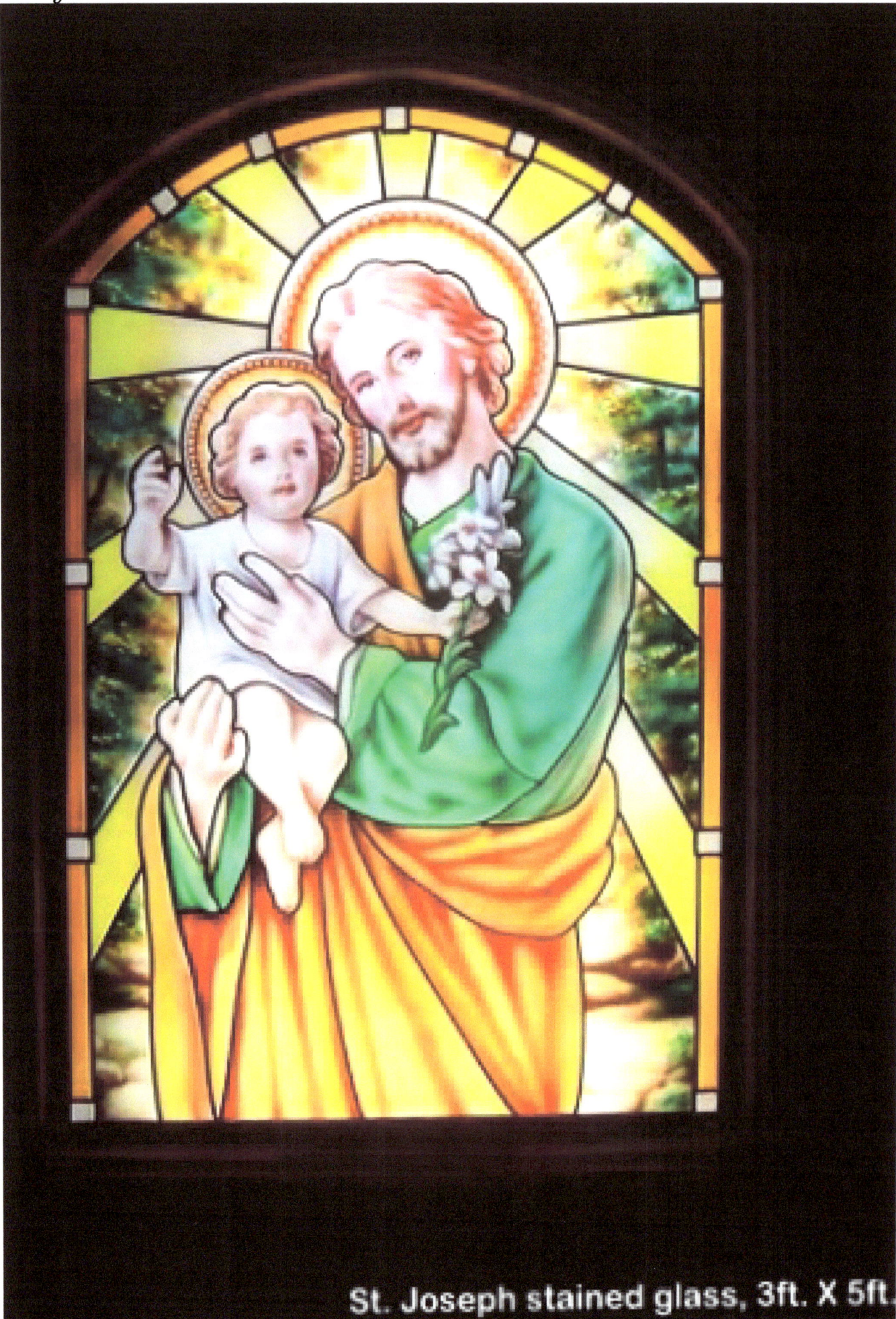

St. Joseph stained glass, 3ft. X 5ft.

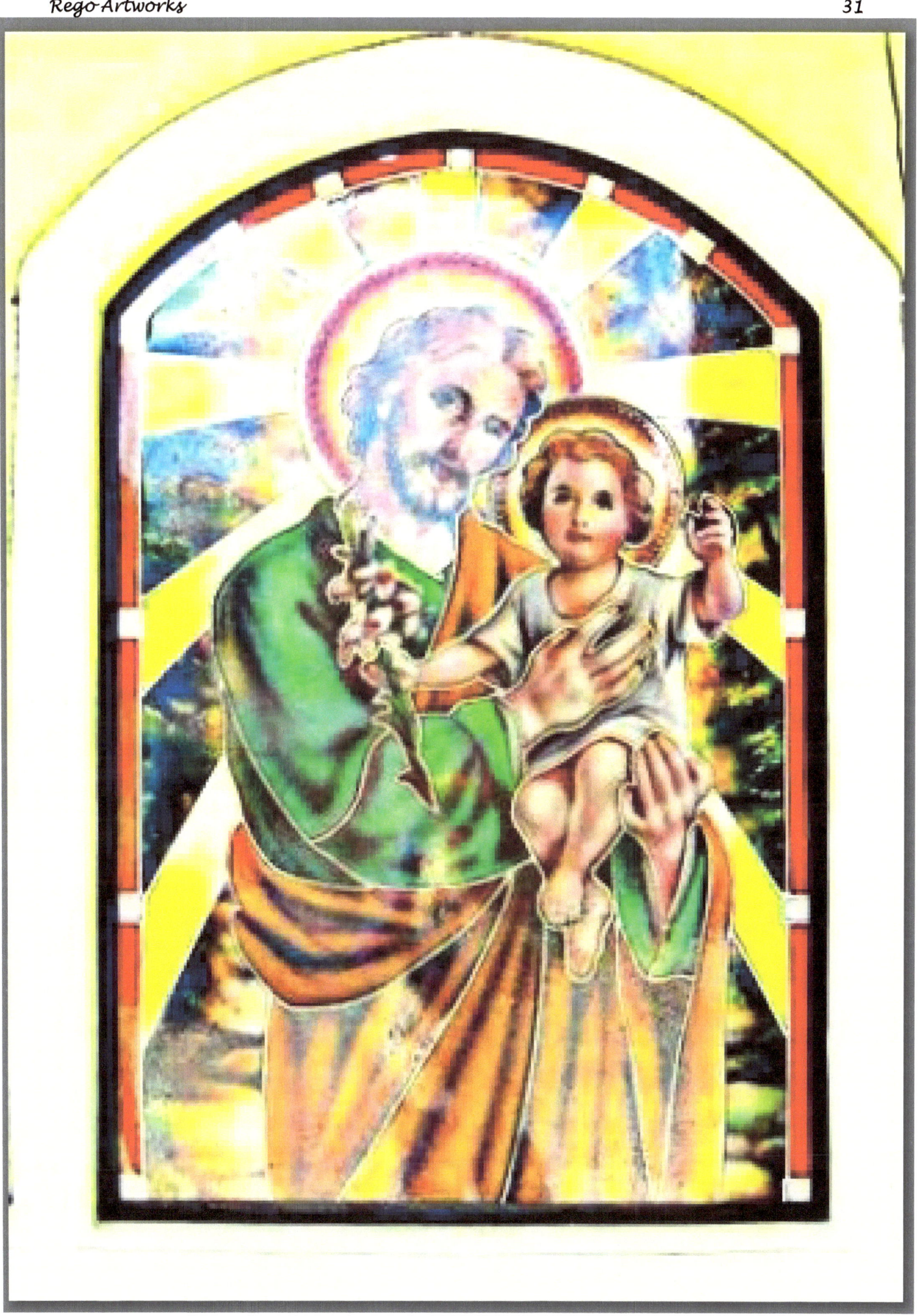

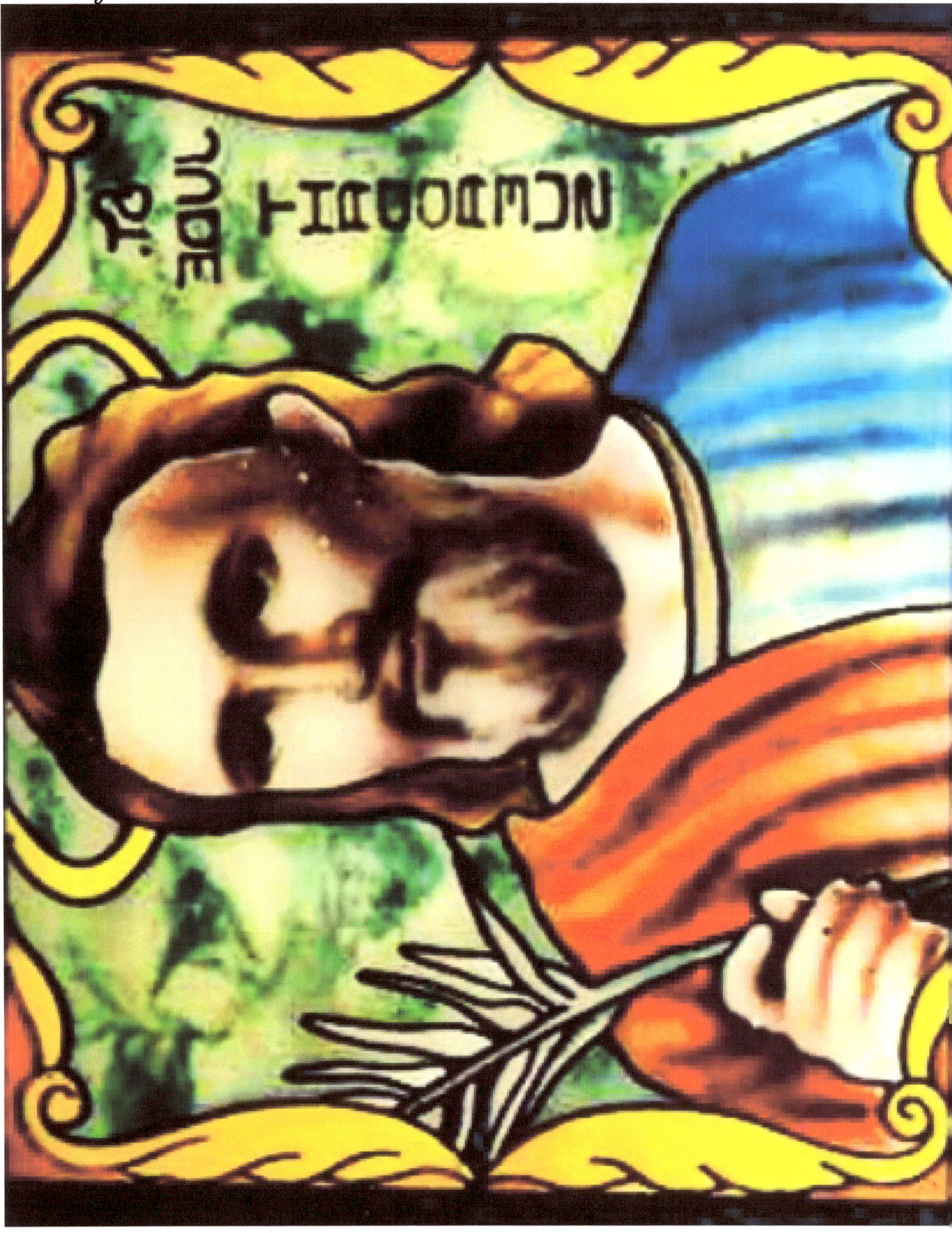

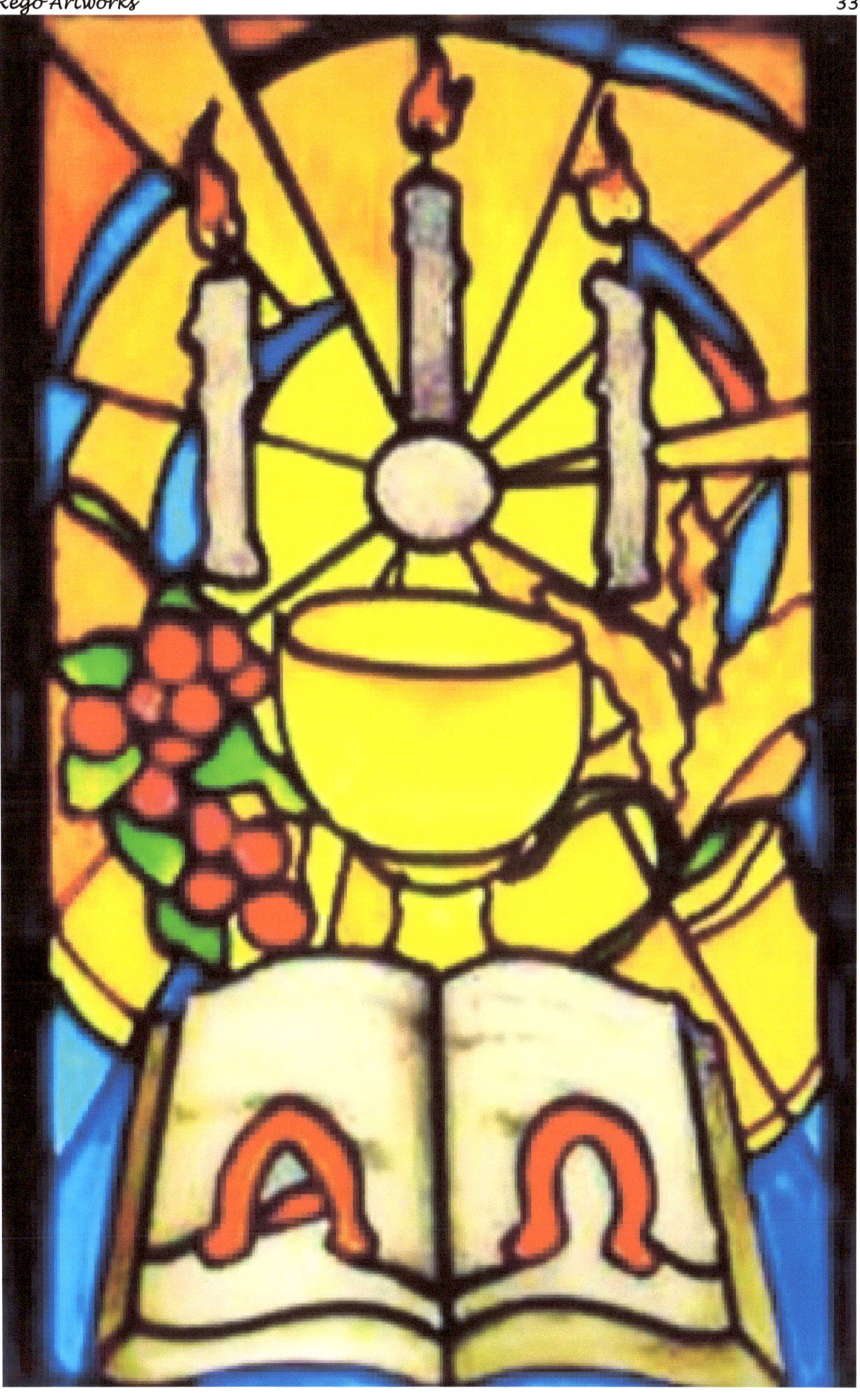

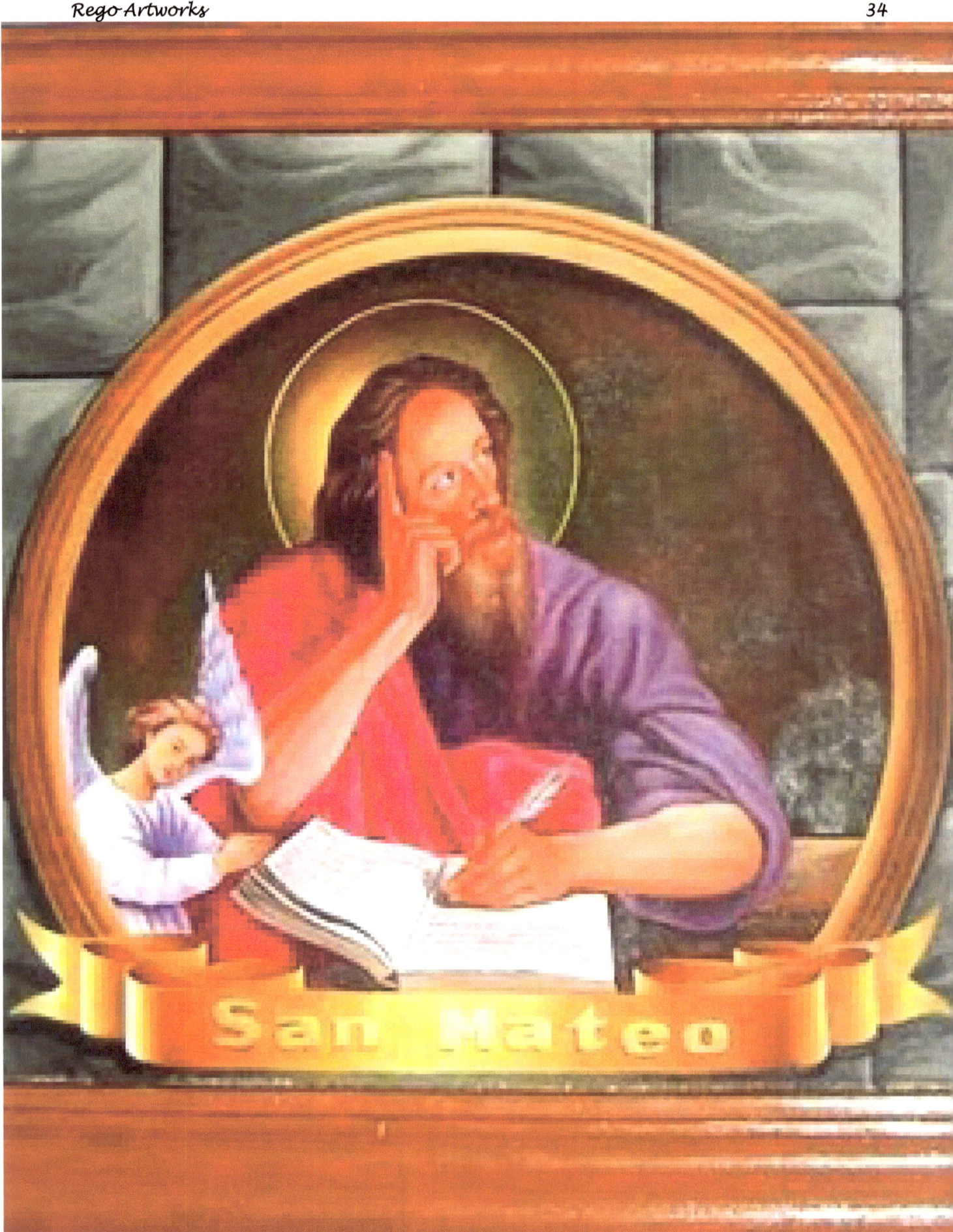

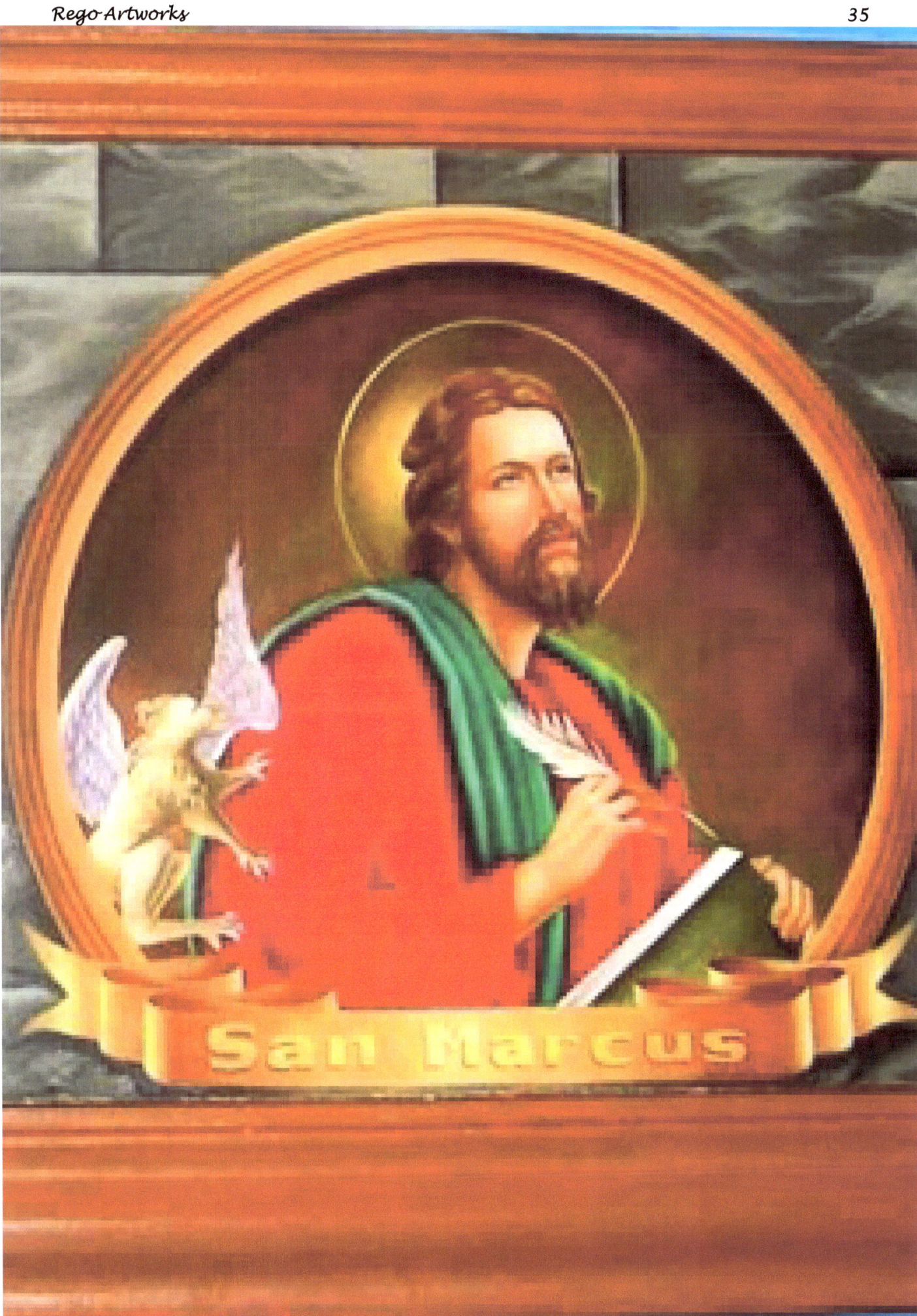

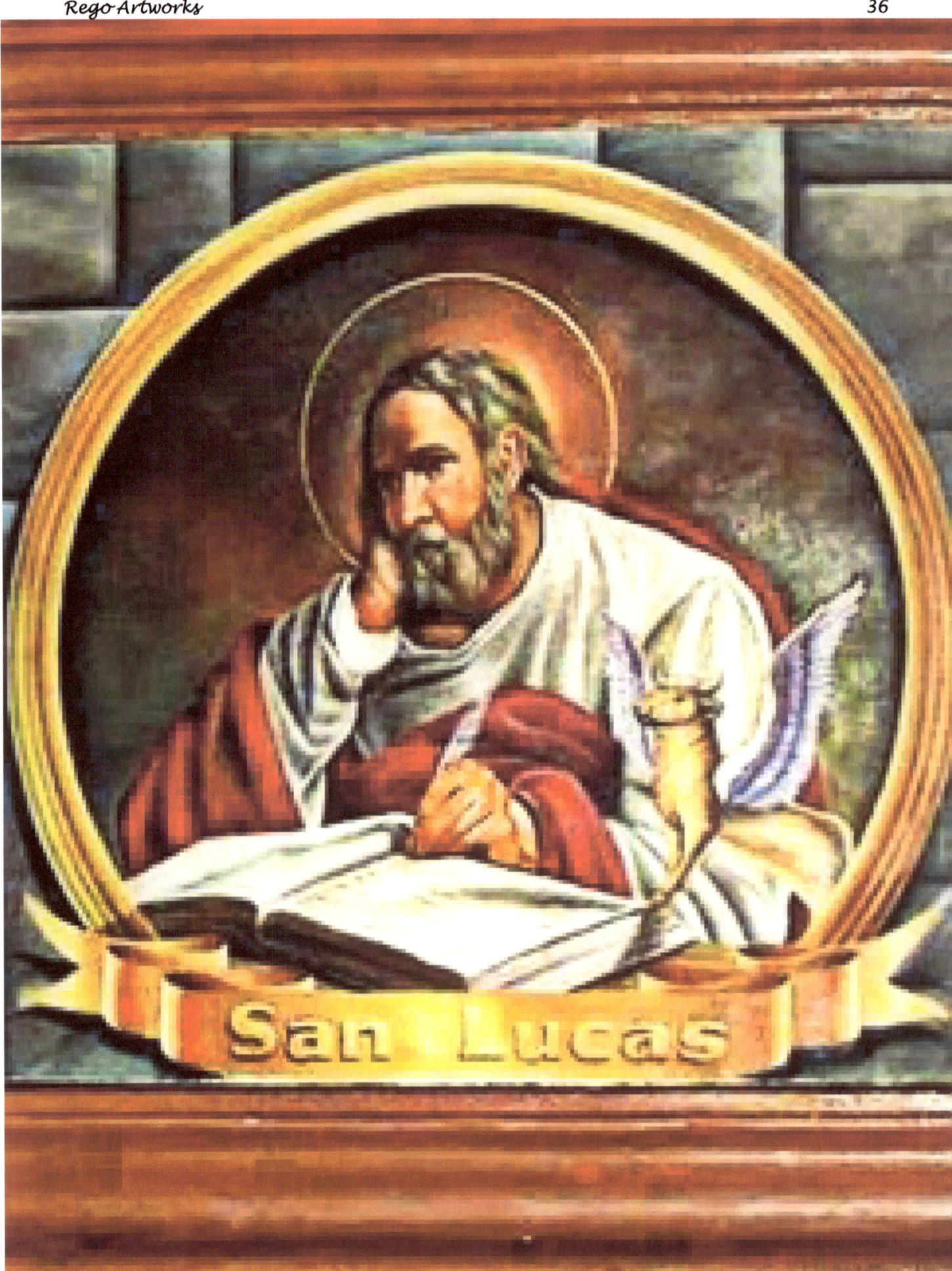

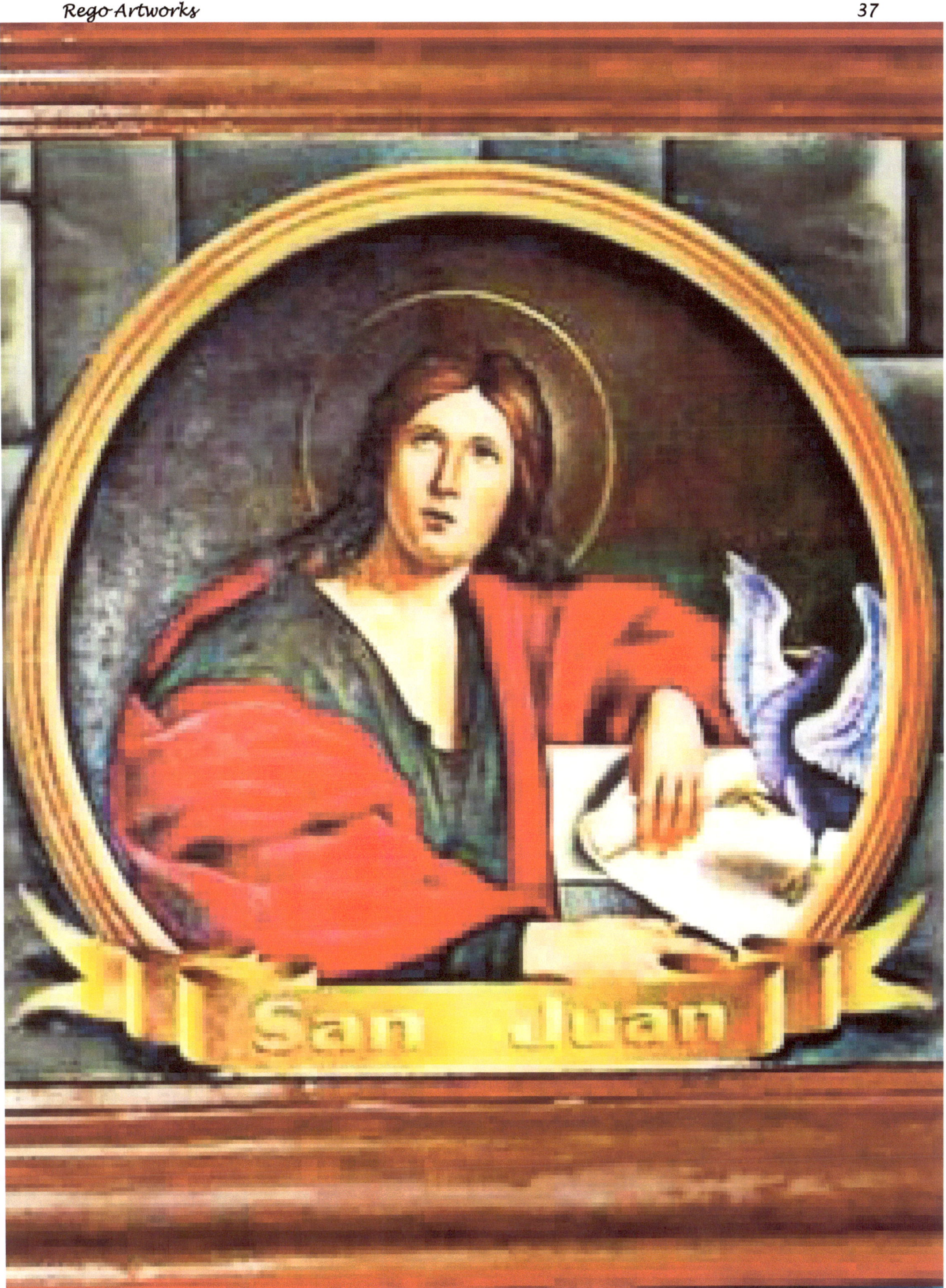

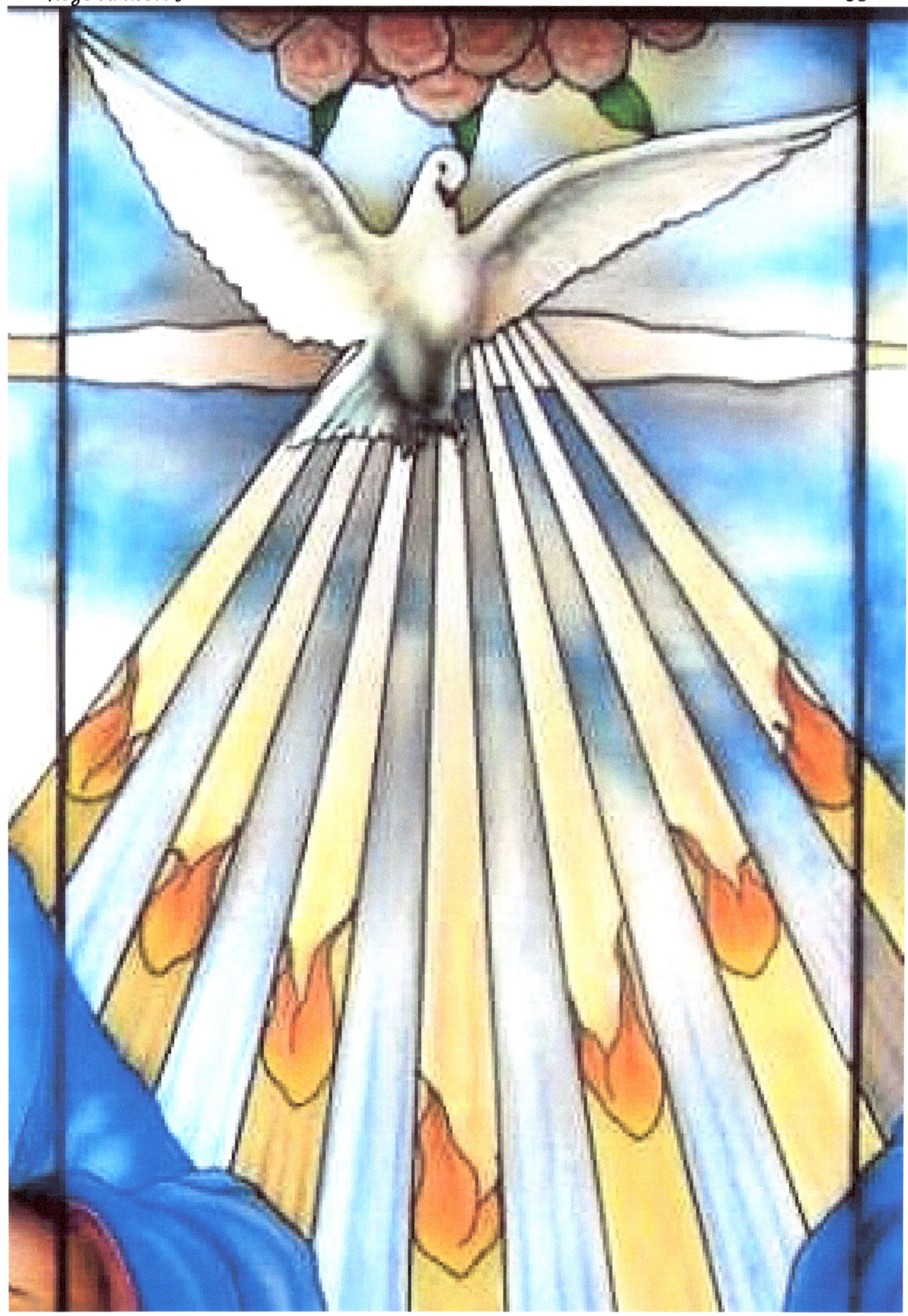

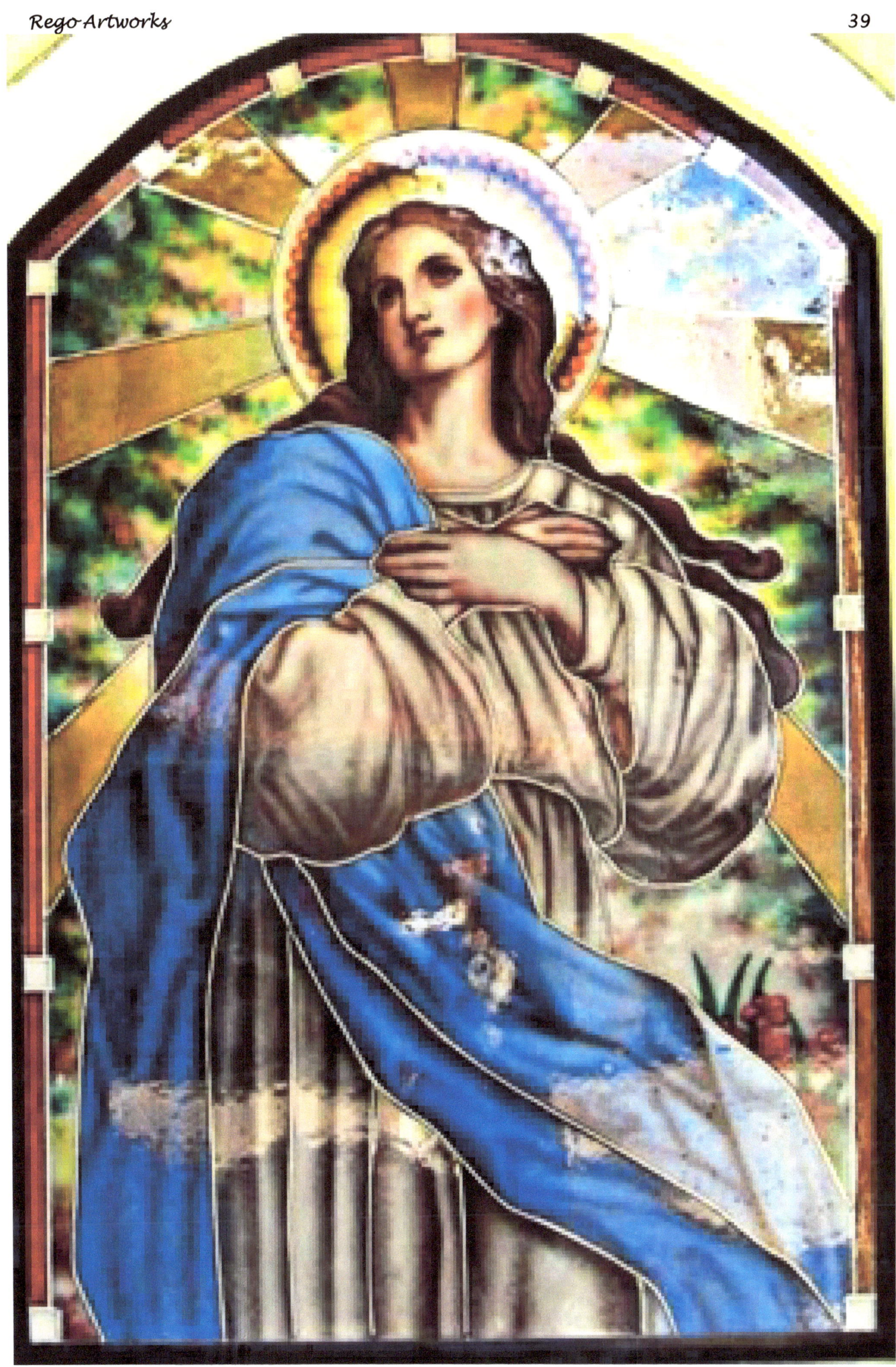

Publisher's List - Buy online as paperback or kindle, contact
job_elizes@yahoo.com, tatay@usa.com

Writings 1 Book, 2012 , Articles by Bambi Harper + Butch Jiimenez + Dr. Phil Stack + Noel Alegre + Toto Causing +_ Melanie Ferrer + Susie Barbieri _ Rodel Ramos + Sylv Salvador + Tatay Jobo Elizes + + **Writings 2 Book, 2012,** Artices by Gov. Grace Padaca + Melanie Aquino + Toto Causing + Rodel Rodis + Cesar Torres + Joey Concepcion Charity Guides + Cesar Lumba +_ Casiano Mayor Jr. + Sonny Coloma + Anonymous.+ + **Writings 3A Book, 2012,** Articles by Norman Madrid + Dr. Rene Azurin + Ernie Delfin Toto Causing + Dr. Jose Abueva + MarVic Cagurangan + Casiano Mayor Jr + Rod Garcia + Roy Gaane + Tatay Jobo Elizes + + **Writings 3B Book, 2012,** Articles by Ceres Busa John Reyes + Bert Guiang. + + **Writings 4A Book, 2012,** Articles by Dr Jose Abueva + Col. Dennis Acop + Fred Natividad + Irineo P. Goce + KaPule2 + Miguel Reynadlo + Marjor Ann Elizes Reyes+ + **Writings 4B Book, 2012,** 1. Mi Ultimo Adios (My Last Farewell), *Dr. Jose P. Rizal* + 2. Aling Pagibig Sa Tinubuang Bayan, *Gat. Andres Bonifacio* + Articles b Irineo P. Goce or KaPule2 + + **Writings 5 Book - "Best Hopes" 2010** (About President P-Noy), Articles by Tony Meloto + F.SionilJose + Juan L. Mercado + OFWs Lette + Marcelo Tecson + Cesar Torres+ Perry Diaz + Dr. Philip S. Chua + Ernie Delfin + Atty. Ted Laguatan + Frank Wenceslao Jaileen F. Jimeno + Tatay Jobo Elizes + + **Writings Book, 2010** + I. SONA - State Of Nation Address - English - *Pres. Benigno Aquino III* + II. SONA - State of Nation Address - Pilipino - *Pres. Benigno Aquino III* + III. First 100 Days peec - Pilipino - *Pres. Benigno Aquino III* + Artiucles by Bert Guiang + Tony Meloto + Felicito or Tong C. Payumo + Cesar Lumba + Flor Lacanilao + Juan DelaCruz or Txtmanika + Dr. Ramc Marquez + Joey Jamito + Percival Cruz + Rod Garcia + Orion Perez Dumdum + Sarah Raymundo. + + **Writings 7 Book, 2010** - My Vintage Pics - Pictorials & Family, Tatay Job Elizes + + **Writings 8 Book, 2010,** Articles by Gel Santos Relos + Ms.Mike Portes + Jose Ma. Montelibano + Tony Meloto + Dr. Philip S. Chua + Dr. Cesar D. Candari + Dr. Elise Serina + Greg B. Macabenta + Irineo P. Goce or KaPule2 + Percival Cruz + Juan DelaCruz or Textmani + Demosthenes B. Donato. + + **Writings 9 Book, April 2011,** Articles b Judge Simeon dumdum Jr + Gemma Cruz Araneta + Larry Henares Jr + Tony Joaquin + Allen Gaborro + Atty. Toto Causing + Mar-Vic Cagurangn + Emily Espanol Derry, Poet + Ely Jean Felarca, Poet + Naysan A. Albaytar + Laura Wade, Blogger + Perter Allan Mariano + Marge Trajeco-Aberasturi + Julia Carreon Lagoc + Irineo P. Goce or KaPulle2 + Anonymou + + **Writings 10 Book, July, 2010,** Articles by Atty.Ted Lagutan + Percival C. Cruz + Allen Gaborro + Peter Allan Mariano + M.L. Munoz + Alvib T. Tabaniag + Resty Odon + D Phili S. Chua + Dr. Cesar D. Candari + Anonymous. + + **Writings 11 Book, August, 2011** + 1, SONA In English and Filipino, by President Benigno Aquino III (P-Noy) + 2, Telltal Signs: SONA and the Dogfight Over Spratlys, by Rodel Rodis + Atty. Ted Laguatan + Tatay Jobo Elizes + Jeremiah M. Opiniano + OFW Journalists + Bob & Carol Hammerslag + Rog P. Olivares + Rob Ceralvo + Anonymous + Irineo P. Goce or KaPule2 + Random. + + **Writings 12 Book, April 2012** + Articles By Orion Perez Dumdum + Julia C. Lagoc Honorio M. Cruz, MD + Ben Gonzales, MD + Mar-Vic Cagurangan + Marisa Lerias + Gerry Partido + Dr. Cesar D. Candari + Erwin De Leon + Jovelyn B. Revilla + Tatay Jobo Elizes + **Writings 13 Book, July 2012** + Articles by Raymundo E. Narag + M.L. Munoz + Sonia Barbara gl Munoz + Pamela Joy Agtoto + Percival C. Cruz + Tatay Jobo Elizes + Jhak Eslit Bayobay + Reygel Saplad Perales.+ + **Timely Writings 14, 2013** + Articles by Cesar F. Lumba + Eugenio Pulmano + Late Jesse Robredo + Antonio Nievera + Alvin Tabaniag + Kevin L. Nadal + Anonymous + Fred Natividad + Anonymous + Ellen Tordesillas + Lat Capt. Rene N. Jarque + + **Timeless Writings-15 (TW15), 2014** + Articles b SC Justice Antonio T. Carpio + Atty Dodel Rodis + Atty. Ted Laguatan + Sona by Pres. Benigno Aquino III + F. Sionil Jose + Dr. Philipi Stack + Racz Kelly, Padilla + Bert Armada. **Timeless Writings-16 (TW16), 2014** + Articles about The Martyrs of Camarines Norte + by Rodel Rodis + R.A.Gubalane + Robert Bernardo + Pres. Aquino's SONA 2014 + + **Timeles Writings-17 (TW17), 2014** + Articles by + Irineo P. Goce or KaPule2 + Rodel Rodis + Julia Carreon-Lagoc + Alvin Tabaniag + Ragubalane + RedButterfly4803 + Cesar Torres

Solo Authored Books: + + +

Book A, **Turning Points,** *Job Elizes Sr,1968 (Reissue 2009)* + + + Book B, **Be Considerate For Once,** *Tatay Jobo Elizes (Jr), 2013* Book C, **Piglets Unlimited - Wealth,** *Tatay Jobo Elizes, 2009* + + + Book D, **Out of the Misty Sea We Must,** *Cesar Lumba, 2010* + + + Book E, **Fulfilled** – *Gonzales Reynaldo, Editor, 2010* + + + Book F - **Reflections** - *Bert Guiang, 2010* + + + Book G, **Writings 7 - My Vintage Pics,** *Tatay Jobo Elizes, 2010* + Book H, **May Bagwis Ang Pag-ibig,** *Percival C. Cruz* + + + Book I, **Letters To Matrimony,** *Irineo P. Goce, Ka Pule2, 2011* + Book J, **Songs I Wish You Knew,** *Soledad R. Juan, 2011* + + + Book K, **Make My Day,** *Larry Henares Jr., 1993, Re-issue 2011* + Book L, **Our Guerrero Family,** *Tatay Jobo Elizes, 2010* + + Book M, **Handy Jokes,** *Tatay J. Elizes, 2011* + Book N, **FaveArt 1,** *Tatay Jobo Elizes, 2011* + + Book O, **Beyond idle thoughts,** *MLMunoz, Sept,2011* + + + Book P, **Cracks In The Armor,** *Mariano Ngan, Oct 2011* + + + Book Q, **FaveArt 2,** *Tatay Jobo Elizes, 2011* + + Book R, **Balitang Kutsero,** *Perry Diaz, Jan 2012* + + + Book S, **FaveArt3,** *Tatay Jobo, 2011* + + Book T, **FaveArt4** *,2012, Tatay Jobo* + + Book U, **Stack Family Journals,** *Phil & Fe Stack, 2012* + + + Book V, **Emily, An Adoption Journey,** *Romerl Elizes, 2012* + + + Book W, **Hermes Alegre Art Gallery,** *TJ & Hermes, 2012* + + + Book X, **Masaya Din, Malungkot Din,** *Jovelyn B. Revilla, 2012* Book Y, **Tiis, Sipag At Tiyaga,** *Raquel Delfin Padilla, 2012* + + Book Z, **Until I Meet You,** *Jhackie Eslit Bayobay, 2012* + + Book AA, **Buhay At Pag-ibig,** *Argel Lucero Tamayo, 2012* + + + Book AB, **Hail to the Second Best,** *Dr. Philip Stack, 2012* + + + Book AC, **Life Bus,** *Mommy Joyce Pineda-Faulmino, 2012* + + Book AD, **My Candid Musings,** *Monette Dioquino Calugay, 2012* + Book AE, **Tickets to Life,** *Maria Lourdes Jesalva, 2012* + + + Book AF, **The Dove Files,** *Mike Portes, 2012* + + + Book AG, **Nursing Vignettes,** *Jocelyn Cerrudo Sese, 2012* + Book AH, **Poor Ba Us,** *R.A. Gubalane, 2012* + + Book AI, **Summer Idyll,** *Avelina Gil, 2012* + + Book AJ, **Legacy (Pamana),** *Rachel Astrero, 2012* + + Book AK, **Narratives Old & New,** *Avelina J. Gil, 2013* + + Book AL, **Buhay Saudi,** *Adele J. Esic, 2013* + + Book AM, **Buhay Ofw Atbp,** *Jessica Napat, 2013* + + Book AN, **Mga Tula Ng Buhay,** *Angelita C. Esguerra, 2013* + + Book AO, **Not by Bread Alone,** *Judge Lily V. Magtolis, 2013* + + Book AP, **Jokes Collection-2,** *Tatay Jobo Elizes, 2013* + + + Book AR, *My Writings Sometimes, Tatay Jobo Elizes, 2013* + + Book AS, **Sa 'Yo Na Ako,** *Shayne A. Martinez, 2013* + + Book AT, **My Kin's Family Trees,** *Tatay Jobo Elizes, 2013* + Book AU, **Rizal Family Tree & Others,** *Tatay Jobo Elizes, 2013* + + Book AV, **Make My Day-2, Nice & Nasty,** *L. Henares, 2013 (1993)* + + Book AW, **Make My Day-3, Cecilia, Love,** *L.Henares, 2013 (1993)* Book AX, **Handy Lyrics-1,** *Tatay Jobo Elizes, 2013* + + Book AY, **Ang Biblos,** *Rev. Dr. Eugenio Guerrero, 2014 (1929)* + + Book AZ, **Make My Day-4,** *Sweet & Sour, L. Henares, 2014 (1993)* + + Book BA, **Life's Journey, True Stories,** *Dr. Phil Stack, 2014* + + Book BB, **Gerry Gil Writings, 2014,** Danny Gil + + Book BC, **Mr. President,** *Hermie Rotea, 2014* + + Book BD, **Nostalgic Pics 1,** *Tatay Jobo Elizes, 2014* + + Book BE, **MakeMyDay-5, Saints & Sinners,** *Henares, 2014 (1993)* + + Book BF, **MakeMyDay-6, Villains & Heroes,** *Henares, 2014 (1993)* + + Book BG, **Nostalgic Pics 2 (ElizesClan),** *TatayJE, 2014* + + Book BH, **MakeMyDay-7, Tough & Tender,** *Henares, 2014(1993)* + + Book BI, **MakeMyDay-8, Light & Shadow,** *Henares, 2014(1993)* + + Book BJ, **MakeMyDay-9, Give & Take,** *Henares, 2014(1993)* + + Book BK, **MakeMyDay-10, ToBeOrNotToBe,** *Henares, 2014(1993)* + Book BL,**Emily Forever In Love, Poems,** *Emily Espanol Derry, 2013* + + Book BM, **The Sinatra Songbook,** *Henares, 2014* + + Book BN, **The Gaborro Reader,** *Allen Gaborro, 2010* + + *Book BO,* **Ramon H. Lopez - Art Gallery,** *2014* + + *Book BP,* **Philippines Via Old Pics-1,** *Tatay Jobo, 2014* + + Book BQ, **Ronna Manansala - Art Gallery,** *2014* + + Book BR, **Philippines Via Old Pics-2,** *Tatay Jobo, 2014* + + *Book BS,* **Being Good-A Medley Of Love,** *Dr. Phil Stack, 2014* + + Book BT, **Lifestream Fisherman, A Filipino Odyssey,** *Paul Dalde, Jul2014* + + *Book BU, Kristina Reed Manansala, Art Gallery-1, August 2014.*+ + Book BV, **Hermes Art Gallery-2,** *Sep2014,* + + Book BW, **Fave Art-5,** *Tatay Jobo, Sep2014* + + Book BX, **Cash & Credits, Make My Day-11,** *Larry Henares, Sept 2014* + + Book BY, **Rise& Fall, Make My Day-12,** *Larry Henares, Oct 2014* + + Book BZ, **Swans& Swine, Make My Day-13,** *Larry Henares, Oct 2014* + + Book CA, **Touch& Go, Make My Day-14,** *Larry Henares, Oct 2014* + + Book CB, **Life& Death, Make My Day-15,** *Larry Henares, Oct2014* + Book CC, **Kiss & Bite, Make My day -16,** *Larry Henares, Oct 2014* + + Book CD, **Good & Evil, Make My Day-17,** *Larry Henares, Oct2014* + + Book CE, **Beast & Beauty, Make My Day-18,** *Larry Henares, 2014* + + Book CF, **Beggar& King, Make My Day-19,** *Larry Henares, Oct 2014* + + Book CG, **Trash& Treasures, Make My Day-20,** *Larry Henares, Oct 2014* + + Book CH, **Wear & Tear, Make My Day-21,** *Larry Henares, Oct 2014* + + Book CI, **Why Blame the President,** *Irineo P. Goce, Oct 2014* + + Book CJ, **Angel& Devil, Make My Day-22,** *Larry Henares, Oct 2014* + + Book CK, **Pretty Ugly, Make My Day-23,** *Larry Henares, Oct 2014* + + Book CL, **Salvation & Damnation, Make My Day-24,** *Larry Henares, Oct 2014* + + Book CM, **Don Daniel Maramba,** *Larry Henarez & Edith Perez de Tagle, Oct 2014* + + Book CN, **Hilarion G. Henares,** *Larry Henares & Edith Perez de Tagle, Oct 2014* + + Book CO, FaveArt-5 + Book CP, FaveArt-6, Book CQ, FaveArt-7, Book CR, FaveArt-8 (all Fave Art books *by TatayJobo), 2014* ++ Book CS, **Minsan May Isang Puta,** *Mike Portes, 2014* + + Book CT, **Rego Artworks,** *Rene Boy A. Gooc, 2014* + +

Publisher: Tatay Jobo Elizes was born in Manila, Philippines, in 1934, retiree, now based in NY, busy self-publishing and involved in piglets dispersal programs.

Publisher's List - Contact job_elizes@yahoo.com, tatay@usa.com
My websites: http://tinyurl.com/mj76ccq + + + www.jobelizes.webs.com
"Buy A Book or Gift Somebody - paperback or kindle edition online"

www.ingramcontent.com/pod-product-compliance
Lightning Source LLC
Chambersburg PA
CBHW050357180526

45159CB00005B/2049